You Are a Queen

You Are a Queen
TRANSFORM YOUR PAIN INTO POWER

CELIA ANZALONE BOWERS

Dedicated to:

My loving husband, Dane, whose unwavering support has been my anchor. And to my precious twin boys, Tristan and Preston, whose laughter and joy light my path. The love of my three boys has empowered me to heal and grow into the woman I always aspired to be. My progress and achievements have been intertwined with their presence and influence.

This book is a testament to our journey together.

Table of Contents

Foreword 1

Note to Reader 6

Introduction: You, Center Stage 9

Chapter 1: You Deserve the Fairytale, Too 15

Chapter 2: You May Fool a Judge, But You Can't Fool Yourself 20

Chapter 3: Little Princess Lost 37

Chapter 4: Finding Grace in Surrender After a Dark Night of the Soul 54

Chapter 5: Patience Is a Virtue 79

Chapter 6: A Queen Forgives Herself—Making Peace with Your Shadow Self 91

Chapter 7: Beauty Is Only Skin Deep—A Queen Takes Care of Herself 101

Chapter 8: Find Your Fire—Do the Impossible 118

Chapter 9: Transform Your Pain into Power 131

Chapter 10: Love Waits for You, Queen 145

Chapter 11: A Queen Walks the Walk 151

Conclusion: Claim Your Title and Wear Your Crown with Pride 157

Epilogue 161

Ending Poem 168

Acknowledgements 179

Foreword

Trauma; mostly known as a painful emotional experience that can cause long-lasting psychological effects with some never recovering. But for Celia, trauma was the challenge she knew she had to overcome. Celia takes you through her childhood that sets her up for a life of hardship. It wasn't until she rediscovered her faith and surrendered to God, that she was led to her new beginnings.

With each story she shares, Celia takes you through not only the events of that moment, but the emotions she felt. As you read, she invites you to open your heart, mind, and soul, delving into each word she writes. With that, doors into your past will begin to open; doors that you may have never known were there. *But why?*

During our lifetime, we all experience some form of trauma. While some have a path leading them to a much darker place than others, each of our souls know what trauma is. Sometimes, we need to listen to and experience someone else's trauma to make this realization. Celia invites you in with open arms to her story, and through this, invites you to think about your past.

As you read, you'll feel the deep pain, sorrow, helplessness, and fear that once filled Celia's body. You'll want to scream for help on her behalf, wish pain upon her abusers, and want to embrace her while saying, *"you are loved."* But by the end of the book, your eyes will be flooded with tears. Not of sadness, but of joy as your body senses a rush of peace.

You see, each of us has a story to tell. It's just a matter of who's willing to put their fears and pride behind them that come out on top. Celia is a miracle and a gem this world must protect. Through her story, she's healed hundreds, if not thousands of tired and beaten souls. Because of her courage to drop the shield, we can collectively come together and fight her fight; one she's done alone for way too long.

Have you ever thought of what life could be like if you let your demons free? Let the shame, misery, and addiction leave your body and never return? It's something that little Celia had always dreamed of, but never thought was possible. With her trauma beginning at just two years old, she felt as if there was no way out; no way of escaping the vicious cycle she was going to live for the next 30 years. But one thing little Celia kept with her was her unwavering strength and will to never give in. It was a gift that so many would question: *how*? But, when you are just two years old, screaming at the top of your lungs, hoping that someone, anyone, would hear you, strength is all you can rely on.

Celia's story isn't about just one instance, but she takes you through multiple modes of the trauma she's faced. For someone who hasn't experienced a trauma so deep, so raw, and so painful, you may be reading and not fully understand. But, she takes the time to go back to the scientific evidence, explaining trauma in a way that translates to everyone. She explains the why behind the trauma and the responses one may have in any given moment. It's as if she is right there, whispering in your ear, the meaning behind her words.

My connection to this book all began because of the Mrs. International pageant of 2024. I was Mrs. New York International 2024, arriving in Tennessee for the national competition, not knowing really anyone. On the first night, at our Lisa Dean Welcome Party, Celia, who was Mrs. Tennessee International 2024, welcomed me to the table she was standing at. We must have talked for at least an hour that night, laughed, and shared our excitement for the upcoming competition. It was at that moment, that I knew I had met a friend for life. But she's more than a friend; she's a sister. Bonded together through pageantry, our stories of philanthropy, and a life we are willing to share with the world.

It wasn't until I heard Celia's 30 second speech during rehearsal one day, that made my jaw hit the floor. I had no idea the extent of which she's experienced, but I knew it was something that was so traumatic, it changed her life forever. I never had the courage to ask Celia exactly what happened while at the competition. We spent the next week, day in and day out, together, not bringing up that 30 second speech. On finals night, I had the honor of standing next to her amongst the top five; placing 3rd Runner-Up myself, and Celia, 1st Runner-Up. For a moment, I thought I had the courage to ask her, "why," but quickly erased that from my thoughts.

Her speech haunted me for the next month in a way I can't even describe. I had to know more, I had to ask, "why," because deep down, I knew there was a reason. Celia and I had a connection that I now see after reading her book. Doors about my past flew open, feelings I stowed away came flooding back, and fears I once had, felt present again. It was all because of her story. She helped me heal in ways I didn't know I needed healing from. Celia made me feel comfort, validation, and love with each word I read. I've learned that you should never underestimate the power of literature and I know you'll experience that feeling after reading this book.

Meeting Celia wasn't a coincidence, it was God's way of guiding me to healing I needed and a safe space to tell all. I welcome you to do the same; read through *Celia's Eyes*, meet her, live her life if only for a moment and see the good that transpires.

We always say, "don't judge a book by its cover." Celia shows just how valid that statement is. First impressions are everything and for her, you'll see a gorgeous mom of two boys, married to an incredible man, living a life one may dream of having. But, Celia peels off those layers as the book progresses and shows you that it wasn't all beautiful; not even close.

This book is one you'll want to keep close, write notes in, and cherish for a lifetime.

Seeing the world through the eyes of such an inspiring individual can change your perspective on life. It's not about the trauma she went through, but the way she was able to turn her life down a path of success. Celia is no longer afraid to be authentically herself and it's a lesson we can all learn.

I challenge you to read this story slowly, thoroughly, and with an open heart. Don't just read the words on the page, but embrace them, feel them, and understand their meaning. In doing this, you're diving into an experience unlike any other. Remember that in order to heal from trauma, you must *transform your pain into power*.

Lexi Spadaro, M.S. ED. in Early Literacy
Mrs. New York International 2024

Note to Reader

Dearest Queen,

Let the words within these pages that resonate be your invitation to heal. You are here and have endured for a greater purpose than you may realize. My hope is that by the end of our journey together, you will have gained a deeper understanding of what that may be.

Together, we will travel back into our hearts. It's important to remember that feeling your feelings for the first time—in a long time—may be part of the healing process for you too. As I have relived my own traumas and poured out my heart on your behalf, I have grieved, I have rejoiced, and I have even more deeply healed.

This is intended for you. Yet throughout this journey, I've found that it's also been for me—and that no one can navigate this path alone.

Promise me, if you don't already have someone to talk to—if it feels too heavy—you will seek support. Do not start reading this book if you don't have at least one friend you can call on if your feelings become too intense. We are on this journey together and you can add me as a resource at celiaanzalonebowers.com. However, a mentor or coach can never take the place of a licensed mental health professional.

I personally see a therapist once a month for maintenance and discuss internal family systems, also known as IFS. IFS was developed by Richard Schwartz and views the mind as made up of distinct "parts." I refer to my wounded parts as children rather than a wounded inner child because it best reflects the idea that I have *multiple* parts representing different experiences and various ages of my vulnerability, trauma, and unmet needs from my childhood. Each of these wounded parts can have unique feelings and memories. Acknowledging them as separate entities facilitates a more nuanced healing process and promotes better integration within the family system. I will discuss this further in chapter three.

As much as the pain from my past has been healed and transformed into a powerful testimony to help heal and empower others, there is still so much my inner wounded children are reckoning with as they courageously continue this beautiful and bittersweet path to healing.

The beginning of my spiritual awakening was on January 21st of 2011 at around 1:00 pm cst. I could say I never asked for this nor was it planned, and only the latter would be true. Less than a week prior, I cried out to God in desperation asking that he "Draw near to me" and I guess we could over a decade later, presume he did just that.

When I first felt led to pour out and share what might help an invisible audience God had placed upon my heart, I had to awaken painful parts from my past. I acknowledged them and gave them their proper respect—a *voice* so they might finally be heard. This was over a decade before I was healed enough to share them aloud—this writing from my heart was a start.

I released tears from the innocent little girl that surprisingly still existed, tears from the broken and battered young woman that I had attempted to bury, and tears of the angry teenager who had been sick and tired of being silenced and shamed. Each of my tears were unique in their expression—with the sound of my sobs spanning between their ages.

I pray you take to heart what I say in my message addressed to you, inspired by the love of someone who cares for you in a way that will never leave you nor ever forsake you. This is me sending back out into the world the same love that healed me—which I pray creates a ripple effect of love that heals you and those you love in your life. We can only help heal the world to the extent our hearts are open to healing ourselves.

You will find that if you are hurting, you have a friend. We are all connected, and I assure you, dear Queen, you are never alone. Sometimes, I know that knowledge is all we truly need.

With Love,
Celia

INTRODUCTION

You, Center Stage

Imagine the spotlight turning to you. Everyone in the crowd roars. Your friends, those both on stage and in the sea of faces below, are brimming with pride. Maybe some are even holding back a little envy through their smiles and cheers. They may be thinking, "I wish that was me."

The host of the pageant hands you the roses, and the former Queen crowns you after placing a sash over your silver shimmering dress draped in a chiffon half-cape. You are the winner! You are a Queen! It's the happiest day of your life, right? You finally have achieved everything you had been working toward for this moment, this day.

Maybe it's not winning a pageant you're dreaming of. Maybe it's graduating college, finishing the marathon you've trained for, or writing your first book. Maybe it's getting married to the man of your dreams or giving birth to a beautiful child. Maybe it's landing your dream job or making your first million as an entrepreneur. Whatever it is, imagine for one moment what it would feel like to finally have everything you've ever wanted. Go on. Do it. Feels marvelous, doesn't it?

Well, it should.

However, on the evening I received my crown at my first pageant in 2021, I felt, in a word, miserable. I would go so far as to say it was the beginning of a deep despair, a total dark night of the soul, a feeling with which I was deeply familiar. I had seen many in my day.

On that particular night, though, a deep sense of unworthiness pervaded my entire body. In fact, my whole body began rejecting the new reality. As soon as I had heard backstage that I was likely the winner, I began to sob. But they weren't happy tears. They were tears of grief, mourning, and shame.

You see, moments earlier, I had poured my heart out to the audience—sharing how I had overcome a drug addiction, a traumatic childhood, and an abusive relationship. I choked up as I spoke and nearly broke down and sobbed on stage. Before that moment where the broken little girl within me was so clearly manifested, I had believed with my whole heart that I had fully healed, that I had come out on the other side of the darkness, and the past was all behind me.

I had come such a long way from where my recovery journey began seventeen years prior at the time. I had a long list of achievements—nationally ranked triathlete, millionaire businesswoman, wife to a beautiful, intelligent, and deeply caring man, mother to the sweetest twin boys—from "trash" to a treasured beauty queen on her way to Nationals in Las Vegas. One would think I might have finally felt like I was "enough."

I am sure most can agree that standing backstage about to be crowned Mrs. Tennessee, I should have been on cloud nine. This is the moment I had been working toward for nearly two decades—to feel free and fully redeemed. But something was nagging and pulling at my heart.

I, the smiling beauty queen, was dying inside. I was holding onto a terrible secret. I didn't feel like I belonged there—anywhere.

A familiar feeling was rising from within: *I don't deserve this. This isn't me. I'm not worthy.* What followed that night was a crushing dark night of the soul. Would any achievement, any praise, any crown ever make me feel whole and complete?

What would it take to feel worthy—to feel like a Queen? Wasn't I a Queen already? The judges and the world seemed to think so.

Many of us are in the same boat. We're earning achievement after achievement. We're chasing fame, fortune, love, security, or just a sense of peace and comfort within our own bodies. But we keep coming up short. No amount of minutes spent on the treadmill, or money spent on nails and hair, or what society deems "self-care" are doing it for us. We *know* there is something more to this life than always striving and achieving, but we can't place our finger on it. The answer always feels right outside our grasp.

This question sent me on the ultimate path to healing and renewal, where I discovered my power and my healing were one in the same. More importantly, that this power resided within me the entire time.

What I have learned is that we are all Queens—myself included—and we don't need to compete in and win a beauty pageant to prove it. As a Believer, we have already received the only crown that truly matters. This feeling of worthiness is to be accessed and is inherent to us all—it is a way of being, an energy—a state of mind. It came back to me when I saved myself and healed my deepest traumas. I became the Queen of my own heart.

I am going to lay out the process it took for me to take myself out the darkest days of my life over the following pages—first as a survivor of childhood trauma, then as an addict, then as domestic violence survivor, and finally as a grown woman reckoning with the lack of self-love and worthiness that was my birthright. You will see how I grew up from being a little princess lost to a woman who *transformed her pain into power.*

Using a combination of medically and scientifically backed treatments as well as ancient spiritual and energetic healing techniques, I will show you how to identify the demons you are running from, fighting, or coping with, and show you a clear path forward.

Through my own stories and the variety of modalities of healing I used to transform, I will help you rethink the stories you are telling yourself, shift your perspective, confront your shadow self, make peace with your inner child, forgive yourself and others, and harness your pain and turn it into your power so you can fully embrace your life and experience a life beyond your dreams.

I pulled myself from the ashes of my self-destructive and trauma-filled life and created beauty, love, hope, and manifested a life beyond my wildest imagination. And now, I want every woman, including you, to know they can too.

Take it from me: No matter what happens to you—you're strong, you are beautiful, you are worthy—*You Are a Queen*.

This is my promise to you—you, too, can overcome anything you have faced or are facing in your lives, and you, too, can shout from the rooftops, "I am a Queen! I oversee my own destiny! I make my own rules! I keep my boundaries firm! I don't back down from difficult feelings or situations. I am no victim, but I have agency over my own life. I am worthy of all the love, joy, peace, success, and abundance life has to offer. I am the queen of my own heart!" That way, when you hear, "You are a Queen," you will only feel overwhelmed with joy for the woman you've fought so hard to become. You will not feel unworthy, you will confidently claim your rightful title, because you have learned from my book how to:

- Get honest with yourself
- Name and understand your earliest traumas
- Realize that your self-destructive behaviors were borne out of a basic need to survive
- Deal with your own dark nights of the soul
- Take ownership of your current situation and take action to heal and recover
- Confront your shadow self
- Discover modalities that heal, and continue to encourage healing
- Forgive yourself and others
- Recognize the importance of compassion—not only for others, but for yourself
- Find your fire—your passion and purpose
- Do the impossible
- Walk the walk—live your life with integrity and intention
- Claim your "title" i.e., your story, birthright, and then rewrite your own ending
- Wear your eternal crown with pride

CHAPTER

One

You Deserve the Fairytale, Too

Something deep within me—an unmistakable voice—was crying out. She was desperate to be heard. This voice, my soul, knew intuitively what I needed to heal. For the first time in my life, through faith and total surrender, I believed it might be possible.

How could I get it all back? Where would I even begin?

My redemption began with a dream—a desperate want for more.

While hoping and hanging on by a thread, I never would have dreamed of the life I live today. My life feels much like the way it did before all the darkness came upon me as a child, but even more divine. As a child, I can recall feeling this beauty—the beauty of innocence.

I had no earthly idea what I could be. There was no way I could discover my true potential while I was dying inside. The light at the end of the tunnel was too far away; in fact, I couldn't even see my tunnel through the darkness that overwhelmed me. I had only heard of one. I only had hope that there was something greater than me to get me through, something greater than myself to revive me back to life.

My mind could barely recall the past feelings of freedom that I felt as a child. The loud and clear voice of the lies that told me that I had done too much, was too far gone for repair, that I was a lost cause, and worthless were all I could hear. My actions during this time reflected my core and limiting beliefs. Can you identify with the experience of feeling burdened by negative beliefs about yourself? If so, this is for you.

The trauma happened to you first. Negative beliefs about yourself emerged. The actions followed.

I wanted to be free from the excruciating psychic pain that made me run away from reality and into the arms of danger—the one caused by the giant, gaping God-sized hole of unworthiness that hollowed me from the inside out. I wanted to be free from the things that I didn't want to do. I wanted to be free from the things that I was desperately drawn to that were going to kill me if I didn't stop.

For years I was running—from myself, from my painful childhood, from facing my truth. The only time I didn't feel crazy or uncomfortable in my own skin was when I was hurting or numbing myself. Only then did my physical pain seem to match my psychic pain.

I knew I didn't want to be addicted to drugs. I knew I wanted a different life for myself and needed to change. I was tired of running, hiding, fighting, and doing everything I could to simply survive each day.

I was a train wreck waiting to happen—a loose cannon about to explode. And that explosion happened, for sure, in the form of eight car accidents in less than a three-year span—four of which were totaled.

When I wasn't feeding the insatiable void with drugs and codependent relationships, the emptiness I felt inside was unbearable. It was more than a feeling inside that left me feeling ugly or unimportant. I was left with a feeling that I was nothing at all. The only emotions that made me feel alive came from the self-destructive behaviors that I felt driven to that made me feel disgusting, mistreated, and abused on every level. But at least then you feel alive, right?

That is why I understand cutters.

Although I was never tough enough to do it well, I did try many times. A cutter has an identity, and so does the "bad girl." We were created to be known and to know others, and I had no idea who I was. And out of the alternatives that I knew, cutting was better than feeling nothing.

Even after I recovered from my drug addiction, I still didn't feel whole. Like so many other women, I thought I needed a man to make me feel worthy of the love I longed for. But all along, that love was there waiting for me to come home to myself. I didn't need someone else to show me the way or to crown me a queen, I found the love deep inside me that helped me begin to truly heal.

After studying our nervous system and doing the intensive work to heal my emotional, psychological, and social well-being from my traumatic childhood, I now understand what led me to that dark path, and why so many others find themselves in the same situation.

Why in the world would a young woman feel the need to hurt or numb herself? Though she didn't realize then what she knows now, little Celia was doing everything she could to survive. When I am talking about my younger, "trashy," out of control self, I am talking about a young girl who saved my life and kept me here on this earth. I am no longer ashamed of her. I honor every piece of her.

One of my breakthroughs in healing was learning to give myself grace and honor the younger versions of myself that stabilized my sanity to the best of her ability while keeping me alive the only way she knew how.

Through intense therapy, medication for a brief season of my life, add in the magic of energetic healing, life coaching, self-healing, and self-work, I finally became fully sober in July of 2022. There was no more reliance on weed or wine, self-sabotaging behaviors, unworthiness, and self-loathing. And I instantly felt led to begin sharing with others that needed a way out the path I paved for them.

After getting sober I soon started my podcast, *Love Waits for You*, where I began to hear from others struggling in the same way. To think that for so long, I felt so alone in this journey, when the truth is I was never alone, and neither are you.

For years, my only dream was to be free. It was a dream that my soul just wouldn't allow to die. But although I dreamed of freedom, I never believed my dreams would one day come true.

Now, I am a believer in fairy tales.

So how can *you* get it all back? Where would you even begin?

Your redemption begins with a dream—a desperate want for more.

Straighten Your Crown Exercises:

- Ask yourself, what is your deepest dream? For me, it has always been freedom.
- Put your dream in writing in your journal. Let your desire for more be the seed.
- In your journal, write how your life would feel compared to how it does now if your dream were to come true.

CHAPTER

Two

You May Fool a Judge, But You Can't Fool Yourself

Twenty years ago, I was shaking in my bed, coming down after years of being addicted to drugs. I was unable to move, feeling paralyzed with trauma, grief, hopelessness, despair, and on the verge of giving up. The only thing I knew to do was to reach out through a short, silent prayer to God: *Help me.* From that first moment of surrender—to today—I have healed and transformed my life.

I was a slave to my cravings. I couldn't stay away from the darkness that was killing me to save my very life. I was addicted to what I called love, and I was addicted to drugs. No matter what I did, I could not break the chains that bound me.

That is, until I could.

Whether it was the most abusive relationship I have ever been in that almost took my life one summer night or the cocaine and meth addiction that brought me to my knees by nineteen years old, within both dark pits my pleas resounded the same. I begged for the Lord to, "Please, help me."

And in both instances, I experienced a miracle.

Although I believe some of us may be more predisposed to developing an addiction than others, one does not just wake up a drug addict. Have you ever wondered what might have compelled them, or you, to try the drugs in the first place? Rather than asking ourselves, "What is wrong with them?" We should think through the lens of, "What happened to them?" Because I can tell you, the first time I saw cocaine I was not only unwilling to try it—I was terrified of it. I was going to an all-girls preparatory school in Chattanooga, Tennessee, when a friend I had spent the night with introduced me to what would one day become an addiction. Although I didn't try the cocaine that they had poured out on the coffee table, I smoked marijuana for the first time that night. I had no initial interest in that either, but I craved belonging at my new school. And after all I had been through and seen over the past year, trying it felt like it was worth the cost.

I was instantly paranoid that every car that drove by their house was the police. When they started pulling apart pens to snort cocaine, my anxiety really kicked in. I knew they could tell I was uneasy, and judgy, because they moved their party of three downstairs away from me. I had already been through a traumatic year on many accounts, but the trauma wasn't dark enough yet for the drugs to stick.

Would you believe I was only thirteen years old attending one of the most expensive private schools in the state of Tennessee when I was exposed to drugs for the first time? And this was over twenty years ago. Let's not be naïve to the fact that they are everywhere.

By seventeen, I had tried cocaine for the first time. I came home that evening and immediately pulled out my diary to write about how much it "scared" me that I enjoyed it *that* much. The thought of using the words cocaine and enjoy in the same sentence brought an uneasy feeling to the surface that I just couldn't shake. That first time the high had lasted hours. I didn't need more than one line, and I didn't feel bad when I came down.

Although I had loved how it made me feel, I still had the fear of God in me. I realized it was wrong. I intuitively knew it could lead me down a dark path. Therefore, when my first serious boyfriend who I had adored didn't want us doing it again, it felt like a relief. I had a reason to never be tempted again.

Six months later, on my eighteenth birthday, his jealousy which led to us getting into a fight had intensified. He had become both physically and verbally abusive. I will always say the verbal abuse, especially as a young girl, was the most traumatic.

After he cursed me out that afternoon as he accused me of cheating on him, which I never had at that point, I rebelliously sought out and bought cocaine without his permission. Little did I know that the action wouldn't hurt him as much as it would try to kill me.

My eighteenth birthday was spent by myself doing this drug—the very thing he was afraid of destroying us. He must have known that it could steal me away from him as he had dabbled in it long before I had. But as any other woman knows who has been verbally abused, it is a slow and silent killer of love. The cocaine just made it easier to break away. Instead of filling the hole with a codependent relationship, that was the day I ran away from him in a desperate attempt to fill the hole in my heart with drugs.

A lot of people refer to cocaine as "the devil," which isn't a lie. Because from that day forward, it had *taken* and consumed me. Life over the next two years became solely about me and my best friend, *cocaine*. No one and nothing else mattered, and as rotten as I felt on the inside, it soon began to show on the outside. I did it a few times a week on average from my eighteenth birthday on April 14th of 2003 until June of 2005.

I had consumed an average of two grams by myself each time I did cocaine after the first year of my addiction. At that time, I would use it and a high would barely even register, or at best, only last a few moments. What began as my first line of cocaine, whose bliss lasted hours upon hours, turned into a vicious addiction to use more and more, without reaching any sort of high that ever satisfied. But even an unsatisfied high was better than facing my truth sober. My life had become even darker and emptier than the reality I had initially begun running away from due to the physical and psychological trauma inflicted upon myself through my heavy drug use.

It didn't take long for me to be approached by an older lady who worked with me at Cracker Barrel to buy a large amount of marijuana because she knew one of the guys I was seeing sold it. Over time, I also began selling this person cocaine to support my addiction. It was a cycle that was now becoming stronger and harder to break.

With the cashier from the Cracker Barrel in mind, at nineteen years old, I bought my first quarter ounce of cocaine. It's the most I had ever bought on my own. As a drug addict, I was thrilled to have that much at once. And for the first part of the night, I savagely got high in my apartment all by myself. I never felt lonely when I was high. With this companion, I never cried.

When it started making me sick, I decided to leave my apartment and go visit some friends. During my drive back to my hometown, I noticed that my vision had become blurred, and I couldn't recognize the numbers on my cell phone. I started to feel nauseous again from the amount of cocaine I had consumed and pulled over to throw up. I felt less high after that, so I did more before getting sick *again*. It felt like a violent cycle of back-to-back "key bumps" while driving down the road and pulling over to vomit green bile because there was nothing left in my stomach.

When I was an addict, as I so clearly was, I rarely ate. Once I got down to 108 pounds on my 5'6.75" frame and my mom's response to seeing me like that was her offering to cook me a steak. I never turned away from her love. I only absorbed whatever she had to offer me with every fiber of my being.

I can still remember how excruciating the minutes between my "hits" of cocaine were once I started. A "hit" is what I called the high that didn't last for long. This addiction wouldn't let me leave and once I started it wouldn't let me stop. It was the only time I felt a fraction of peace, which didn't last long enough before I needed more.

The night I bought seven grams, I got sicker than usual. I was accustomed to doing cocaine, getting sick, and doing more. I was used to throwing up green bile. Getting sick was the norm for me because it made me feel better enough to where I could do more. I had finally found a medicine that hit the spot and successfully distracted me from reality. This is the thing about cocaine; your body is trying to tell you no by constantly getting sick, but your mind is telling you yes, keep going, you'll feel better soon. You're in a constant battle with your mind and body, and a weakened mind always wins.

What was scary for me and was the beginning of my wake-up call, is that my initial plan was to only do one gram by myself and make money off selling the rest. But by the time I ended up weighing it at my friend's house, half of it was gone. I did over three grams by myself. To put it in perspective, I did the equivalent of forty-five lines that night.

The only reason I ever tried methamphetamine for the first time was because I was coming down from cocaine and there wasn't any more of it available. God forbid, you must face the black excruciating hole and come down. I would go through a whole roll of tissue paper, blowing my nose, when I started letting myself come down. I would spend the entire day "recuperating" in bed while my mind was awake, but my body needed sleep. My body would ache and needed rest, but my mind wouldn't allow it. I put myself and my body through misery to stay high. I would do whatever it took to prolong the inevitable, which was coming down. I first gave meth a try in this altered state.

Meth had become my secret addiction because everyone knows how dirty it is. Ironically enough, I still had some dignity at the time and knew that taking it was a bridge too far, even for the most hardcore drug addicts. However, with only one line of it, you would be up and going for two days. I did not go through the same vicious cycle. It was worse on my skin and my health, but I understand those that can't ever get free and why.

Would you like to know what the high of meth felt like? The effects of Adderall if you aren't truly ADHD or taking more than your prescribed dose feels if you do truly need it. They both make you feel paranoid, wide awake, icky, and sticky. It feels as if the toxic chemicals from the drugs have become trapped within your body. Underneath your dirty-feeling skin, the drug is trying to escape and seep out through your pores. It's enough to make one's skin crawl.

In the days that follow, you feel as if you have been run over by a truck because the poison remains trapped inside. The aftermath of methamphetamine was undoubtedly worse than Adderall. But even scientists say to think of them chemically as cousins.

Less than a year later, although I did not hear from God audibly, I did hear in my heart the impression of the words, "Go now," as I stared at the shower drain waiting to be murdered by my "husband." I heard this after I was forcibly thrown into the shower to "Clean up my mess!" which was my blood I was covered in while he continued to assault me. I would ultimately receive an annulment by twenty-one years old.

When I *felt*, "Go now," I didn't waste a second. I left the shower running, tiptoed out of the bathroom, and made my way to my escape with only a towel to cover me. I was about twenty feet ahead of him before he had realized I wasn't in the shower and had begun chasing after me. Had I not escaped the moment I was told to "Go now," I don't believe I would be alive today.

Fast forward over a decade to age thirty-six, I thought I had made it. I had broken free. But I could never forget what it felt like to be so chemically, emotionally, and physically dependent on what was killing me, while feeling unable to stop. Through my faith that could move mountains, I had escaped not only an addiction to drugs, but a relationship that could have been fatal.

I had broken free again—from that which was my former life—or so I had tried. As a successful mortgage entrepreneur, I had even buried my first book I was once proud of, *Celia's Eyes*, that came over me when I was twenty-five years old. My ego was ashamed of my story. I had detailed my past traumas and drug addiction, not understanding their full magnitude or impact on my life or that my healing would be ongoing. But it was a release and the beginning of a future so bright one would need to throw on their shades. A miraculous purging. A long overdue moment in time where I met my highest self and to be quite honest, felt consumed by the heart of Jesus which I desperately needed.

My first book came upon me after leaving church one afternoon feeling so afflicted by my thoughts – telling me I was trash and unworthy of my new "good kid" friends. I had been clean from hard drugs for five years. But the drugs, the lifestyle, and the shame had scarred me in more ways than one.

The paranoia was so severe, that my thoughts felt painful to me. I had graduated college a few weeks prior but was still living at home with no plan to move out. This was due to my irrational fears and paranoia that plagued me when I was left home alone as a recovering twenty-five-year-old drug addict.

Once I made it home after church, in total and utter distress, I bowed my entire body down before the Lord and begged him, "Draw near to me." I began to see two things. One was a vision of a scroll in black and white. I wasn't sure what that meant or what it was about. The other was the man I had been emailing with for over a year—a man I was convinced was my future husband. I only had to get better first. This was a man that was a therapist where I was receiving care. Naturally, I thought the vision meant we would get married. Later I would discover that vision had to be telling me that he was *already* married to someone else. In my fragile and vulnerable state, the feeling of devastation was an understatement when I discovered this. He was the first man since my childhood who had given me emotional support without any strings attached. The emotions and the grief that surfaced were from those of a child.

I felt peace while I prayed and received these visions, but inevitably returned to earth. Five days later, on the Friday following the Sunday where out of desperation I prayed for the Lord to draw near, my writing took a turn. From a journal entry to *something* coming over me and I will even go so far as to say, possessing me, to pour out my heart and my shame and my secrets to an invisible audience that I was convinced needed me.

I shook, I rocked, and I cried as toxins left my body while I purged. The last time my face had become *that* broken out with cystic acne was when I was using meth almost six years earlier. I stayed up until 2 am each night pouring my heart out for the sake of those who needed me. I believe that Jesus placed a calling in my heart to help heal others that day. But I also believe that Jesus took my heart over as I poured out words to help others to also heal me. Because when I had reviewed what I had written while under what felt like a trance, I discovered *He* was writing to *me*. I only had to change the pronouns to make it work for others and become a book.

You will have a family once you are well. He promised me among many others.

By thirty-six years old, God's promises to me had been fulfilled. I had met and married a man who was more than I could ever dream up. That's just how God works. We had moved into our dream home with our infant twin boys. I was a very successful mortgage entrepreneur—a hustle hard, "boss babe." I had been through the ringer, but no one would ever know from the outside and I sure wasn't going to tell them. And so, Jesus was right. Over the years, I became mentally "well," enough, to finally find, attract, and marry the man of my dreams and build a family whose love for me soothed my soul. My husband's love, specifically, helped me heal. His love supported me into becoming the whole, worthy, and secure thirty-nine-year-old woman writing to you today.

Now that all my dreams of the past had come true, why did I still feel like I was at war? I woke every morning feeling the peace and predictability of my newfound family life and it set me into a panic. My body and nervous system did not know what to do with peace, happiness, and security. All it had known was chaos.

So I recreated the drama—by drinking.

It had started during what one may refer to as my postpartum depression. I was on the way to my first sales meeting when my twin boys were six weeks old, and I had the desire to drink at 9 am. The level of social anxiety I had felt, along with this new craving, alarmed me. But deep down, it was a feeling I knew all too well.

Eventually, I'd leave the babies with the nanny, head over to the country club "to work" by the pool, and soon I would find myself ordering drinks during the day. I knew what I was doing wasn't good for my family. Deep down, I realized my drinking had turned into an issue.

I am ashamed to admit that it soon became such a problem that I would drive and put other lives at risk while drinking. But even worse? There were times the nanny would get off work at 5 pm at our country club where we paid her to help me watch the twins, and I would drive myself and the boys the 4.6 miles home down backroads completely numbed out. I feel so much shame washing over me as I admit this. What kind of mother would put their own children in danger like that? A hurting one would.

After I had the boys, it didn't take me long to gain the motivation to lose my baby weight. I had become an Orangetheory superstar and had begun competing in triathlons again. I had even placed in the top three of my age group during a triathlon state championship and was headed to my first Nationals competition in Milwaukee. I was making more money in the mortgage business than I could ever dream. The money and the achievements coupled with the binge drinking had become my new, much more socially acceptable drugs.

But underneath it all, there remained a nagging hole because no level of performance could fill it. The achievements were only giving me temporary highs, but at least they made me feel something good. So, one evening, as I searched for more and more that I could achieve or do to prove I was no longer that trashy, needy, nineteen-year-old drug addict, I googled, "Mrs. Tennessee," and right then and there, I applied.

The Director contacted me the following day to sign me up as the pageant was only three weeks away. I was also told I needed a "platform." In pageantry, that is a cause a contestant will advocate for. Are you kidding me? I was called for this. *Now is my time to unbury the book and share my story,* I thought. I found a place where my past would not only be welcomed but revered. And for this I will always know God led me to pageantry to further heal.

Just like my book forced me to meet myself, pageantry did as well. I unearthed the book and my voice and shared with each judge during my first pageant all I had overcome.

And they still crowned me.

I had so many masks I had been hiding under and now beauty queen to add to that list. I had the judges fooled into believing I had healed enough to think highly of myself when deep down, I *still* hated myself. But how could that be with my picture-perfect life?

Here is the deal. We are all lying to ourselves. In fact, right now there is something you're also avoiding. There is something you're scared to face.

We're all out here in the world wearing a mask of some sort. We all play roles—the doting wife, the boss babe, the mom with all her ducks in a row, the beauty queen with perfect hair, nails, and body—if only for "pageant week." But there is something we're avoiding. There is something we're scared to admit—to anyone, let alone to ourselves.

That, my Queens, is the very thing causing us shame. It's causing us to feel unworthy when we receive our proverbial crowns.

That is the thing we are running from when we can't sit still, or we're escaping with alcohol or food. It is what we are avoiding when we are frantically cleaning the house, losing ourselves in a Netflix binge, or my preferred trauma response—running from our demons in a race. It is what makes us anxious and keeps us up at night.

It could be your finances. Are you chronically late on your bills? Are you secretly hiding purchases? Are you hoarding? Are you picking at your skin? Are you taking drugs? Are you overeating? Overspending? Overexercising? Are you working nonstop? Starving yourself? Are you avoiding certain people and situations? Are you comparing yourself to others on social media? The list is endless.

But you are not alone. Everyone is hiding something.

When I interviewed for the title of Mrs. Tennessee, I fooled the judges into finding me worthy when I truly did not find myself worthy. The truth of how I felt about myself manifested in countless ways prior to the pageant and afterwards, but I remained on the run from myself, and I couldn't see it until I was forced to.

Any time I have won or lost within my three-year pageant journey, I have either felt complete peace or devastating turmoil depending on where I was in my journey to self-worth and healing.

Would you believe the most painful was the only evening I was ever crowned? Do you know the thoughts that flooded my mind while being crowned Mrs. Tennessee in 2021?

You are trash. They don't know who you really are. You do not deserve it. You are not worthy. You may have fooled the judges, but we can't fool ourselves here.

Over the eleven weeks that followed as I prepared for my first national pageant, tears of grief, mourning, and shame would come over me when I was alone, often driving. I would have to pull over to convulse and cry.

I shared with my husband these episodes, and because of him knowing my whole story, he was able to feed me the logic my brain needed. He said, "Well, I can see why this must feel overwhelming for you. You have spent all these years thinking poorly about yourself. And now you have people fawning over you. I am sure it can be a lot to process."

Ok, great, I felt, *so I am not going crazy.*

But in a sense, I was.

You see, when your whole body is rejecting a brand-new reality, it is called cognitive dissonance or better known as imposter syndrome. For me, I am not a fake or a phony, so I was on my way to a nervous breakdown. Feeling like a hypocrite or a fraud is my greatest nightmare because of all the religious trauma I experienced as a child.

I now know that God was preparing me to be broken down, and back on my knees, again, to fulfill his grand plan of me experiencing complete freedom in my life. My heartbreaks to come would indeed be my rescue. I was back on my destined path.

Straighten Your Crown Exercises:

- Get real with yourself, for example, do your actions and behaviors match your words?
- Make a list of the things you are lying about to others.
- Reflect on something you are deeply ashamed of.
- Journal about your shame, why you are ashamed, why you lie, and consider if you can stop or not. Ask yourself, "Is it an addiction—which may require outside help?"
- Make a commitment or promise to get honest with yourself and an accountability partner, therapist, 12-step group, or a coach.

CHAPTER

Three

Little Princess Lost

The body keeps a score of each of our traumas, regardless of whether we were too young to remember or how we may have tried to bury them. Although I don't consciously recall chasing my dad's car down my grandparents' pea gravel driveway when he would drop me off from his visitation, my heart and my subconscious do. I was a beautiful blonde-haired, green-eyed baby who must've hated to see her daddy leave her not understanding how he could or why he would.

On Christmas Eve of 2023, my dad and his wife of thirty-seven years—the only active mother in my life—were visiting my family for Christmas. I shared with them the TEDx talk I had prepared for NYC the following month. I physically broke down and let my emotions take over during my talk. At that time, we shared moment of healing.

Over the course of twenty years, there have been numerous instances where healing has brought us together.

Although supportive of my dreams to help others, my heavy past hasn't always been easy for my dad to process. I am his daughter and now that I have my own children, I understand because their pain is also mine. But then my healing has also been his as we share an unbreakable bond.

That evening, I was hit by a truth so thick that I now understand retraumatized me—sending me straight to bed in a freeze state, one of the four trauma responses. If you have been there, you know exactly what I am talking about. It isn't a mood, but a thickness of dark heavy matter that is almost paralyzing. All I feel like doing in those moments is stare into the darkness. I don't cry because I can't even move.

Every Christmas Eve, my family and I deliver gifts and hugs to the residents of a local nursing home. If it weren't for that commitment, I don't know how long my funk would have lasted. It could have ruined the time left to be spent with my parents. I believe these trauma responses are often misdiagnosed as mental health disorders as these feelings can last for years when left unacknowledged and untreated. But that evening taught me an invaluable lesson—that serving others is one of the cures to alleviating our trauma responses.

Serving others feeds us. And it feeds us first.

So, what was this truth that had shaken me to my core? One afternoon in Florida when I was a baby, as my dad was busy at work and without his knowledge, my mom packed everything up, including me, and moved us to Tennessee. My whole life it felt like my dad abandoned me, but the reality was, we had left him. In fact, I was *taken* from him. I had never processed the trauma of being suddenly removed from my father until Christmas Eve of 2023.

He was in the middle of his residency for medical school at the University of Florida which is where I was born. But without hesitation, my dad uprooted his life and transferred to the University of Tennessee to be near me. I now see and *feel* that he tried to fight for me. And I can't imagine how he suffered.

As soon as my mother arrived in Tennessee, she went straight to chasing her same crush from high school who had always played mind games—telling her he would call as she would wait by the phone anxiously all day as a teenager for him to never do so. He might have even told her he cared about her, but his actions said he couldn't care less in high school. He had power over her because she could never catch him. All he had to do was "ask about her" to a friend who felt it was appropriate to relay the message while she was married to my dad, and on an impulse, she escaped her present reality to pursue a new one.

One could say running away had become a part of my DNA. Truly. Have you ever heard of epigenetics? It is a field of science that studies how our environment can impact our genes. Our traumas can't directly alter our DNA sequence. However, they do have significant effects on gene expression and how our genes are read and regulated.

The best analogy I have heard says to think of our lives as a book and our DNA as the alphabet. The alphabet doesn't change. However, the plot within each of our books is fluid and shaped by our experiences. Significant trauma can cause "plot twists," and although it doesn't alter the letters in the alphabet, it is proven our trauma can influence how our genes are expressed. This could negatively impact our moods, how we relate to the world, and our relationships. Trauma can even affect our health and predisposition towards diseases.

But what is beautiful about this study? Those of us who have been negatively impacted by trauma are in more control than we may realize. Studies even beyond my own life have shown that epigenetics can be reversible. Just like trauma can have a negative influence on our genetic expression, the more we are exposed to positive events in healthier environments, our genes are equally impacted for the better. My goal for each of us has been to *not only* fully process our *old* stories, but additionally, find as many *new* ways to feed ourselves with so much love and life-giving experiences that we may drown out the darkness by rewriting our endings full of light.

Does the desire to pursue the guy who doesn't want you sound familiar? I know it does for me. My mother also felt abandoned as a child by her father. And until we heal, we spend our lives unconsciously recreating or reliving traumatic events in an unconscious effort to process and gain control over those situations from our past—essentially reenacting the trauma until we can hope to win and feel like we finally "got it right." That's why in psychology they refer to it as "reenactment."

I was too young to remember anything about my parents' relationship. I don't know what it felt like to live with her overwhelming emotions. I easily forgive her for leaving my dad in the way that she did because I have never walked a mile in her shoes.

My dad eventually moved to Pennsylvania when I was five years old with my stepmom and new baby brother, which meant I only got to see him in the summer and on holidays. It also meant I had to take a plane to visit. I was only five years old when I flew by myself for the first time.

I was told my dad would be flying beside me on the plane from Chattanooga to Pennsylvania. It was only right before I boarded when my mom told me he wouldn't be coming, and I panicked. This wasn't the beginning of my abandonment wound—that wound began when we were torn apart. But it was triggered then.

There was a woman who reminded me of my Nonna, his mother and my grandmother (in Italian), who helped to soothe me, by taking my mind off my panic and drawing me a birthday cake with six candles for my upcoming birthday. She provided me with something I desperately needed: a sense of safety and belonging, one of the most foundational requirements for a person to heal. Throughout my life, I have been drawn to those who recreate that sense of safety and kindness.

The reality is that grandmother helped distract me and made me feel safe, but she could not possibly heal the trauma within me that caused the panic in the first place. That is only a job I could do. The deep work didn't happen for years—not until after my breakdown at the Mrs. Tennessee pageant.

Many of us have deep wounds or traumas that have affected us from early on. I never felt loved or that I belonged. I am not saying my mother and father didn't love me. I am saying: I never *felt* loved, which is different. They were incapable of loving me in the way I, *little Celia*, needed to be loved.

I can't recall the details of my infancy, but I do know I must not have been held enough. I was told when I was hungry my mother would trick me into drinking water sprinkled with sugar so I wouldn't gain any more weight. She was afraid I was getting "fat." She bragged on this logic, so as a child I never questioned it. You can't help but trust those who feed you and clothe you, even if they are wrong. She always said if you started out overweight as a baby then you will likely be overweight as an adult. Knowing this may be true, I had always thought she had done me a favor until I had my own children. Then, I found that when my children were hungry, cold, uncomfortable, or had a desire to be held, it was my motherly instinct to do my best to meet their needs—unless I had been drinking. And then I shape shifted into my sober mother who had checked out emotionally.

Every child has a need for co-regulation. It is apparent this need of mine was never met. Co-regulation is where one nervous system supports and calms another. It happens when a parent is attuned to a child. Being attuned is simply being fully present. It is looking your child in the eyes. It is being with your child during their stressful emotions. It is a tuning into their emotional state instead of ignoring them.

To feel safe and secure as a child is crucial—so they feel seen—or they will spend the rest of their lives searching for this need to be met by others.

This struggle with attunement to one of my children, Tristan, was a big motivator for me to quit drinking. I could not repeat the cycle of causing trauma by way of neglect and live peacefully with myself. I could see into the future by being painstakingly aware of how it had shaped me. I realized that I could regain control over what was creating distance with my children—by quitting alcohol altogether.

When my mom moved us to Tennessee, the boy from high school who she left my dad on a whim for was homeless. He would eventually be brought back to life by way of his mother, and mine, who "loved" him. This man eventually became my "daddy," too. And he also fathered two of my siblings I love dearly.

I can recall my first stepdad being very jealous and trying to push my "real dad" out of my life. There was a time my aunt told one of his friends who was giving me a compliment, "She has her daddy's eyes," referring to my dad. Although true, it ended up costing her time with me when my stepdad found out. From that day forward, he forbade my mother from allowing me to see my aunt without "supervision." I was three at the time, but I remember the conversation because I am the one who brought it up one Sunday after church at his mother's. My mom said every jaw at the dinner table dropped. But it was true, and I knew it then too. I do have my daddy's eyes.

I was often manipulated by both my mom and my stepdad. One weekend as I was headed out to visit my dad, my stepdad asked me in front of my mother, "Would you rather go visit *him* or go fishing with me?"

I immediately asserted, "I would rather go fishing with you."

He proclaimed, "See, she wants to stay with me!"

A major argument erupted between him and my mom in the center isle of their first business together, a carpet store. Over the years, I witnessed several heated shouting matches in front of their employees, and I'm certain there were many more that I didn't see.

My mom always encouraged my relationship with my "real dad." Although my stepdad may not have been my biological father, he was the only one I interacted with on a daily basis. He was more nurturing than my mother, and we spent a lot of quality time together. So yes, as a little girl, I would have chosen him.

I didn't perceive life as challenging during my childhood, despite having gone through trauma. I had two dads, two moms, two Christmases, four sets of grandparents, and two families—one of which I felt completely at home. As dysfunctional as it was—which I didn't realize until I had begun healing in my 20's—I always felt the most comfortable with mother and my stepfather who had convinced himself I was his. I had more freedom than any child typically should, and I relished it as much as any other kid would. But the truth is, I had carried an abandonment wound, which deepened even further when my mom and stepdad divorced by the time I was thirteen. It didn't matter who left whom.

They were there and then they weren't.

I was present, and naturally, felt waves of grief as I mourned at my first stepdad's funeral when I was thirty-five years old. There were photos of us on a slideshow they had displayed despite the fact our relationship had ended over twenty years prior. It still feels odd to have so much history with a man that suddenly left my life after a decade of being my "daddy" without so much as a farewell.

My connection with him—and his family, who had become my own—abruptly ended. It was as if he had died the day my mom drove him away amidst her nervous breakdown. However, it wasn't until his funeral, twenty-two years later, that I was able to process my grief.

I am still healing my childhood abandonment wounds and grapple with irrational fears that those I love might leave. But I have attained something I never had before from doing the deep work of reflecting and facing my pain head on instead of continuing to run away—to alcohol, to relationships, to drugs, and to food.

I have always disliked the saying, "Don't look back, we're not going there." Because what I have come to understand, to transform into who I was created to be, I had to journey back and heal my wounds.

Until we work through our trauma, it keeps us stuck in the past. This limits who we can become. Healing my trauma has resulted in feeling completely safe within my own skin. I now have the capacity to look after myself, my inner healing child and let's be real, children. I may still experience challenging emotions and irrational fears, but they happen less frequently as time passes.

What I hold now, that I didn't always possess, is the unwavering assurance that I will always be ok.

The discomfort in healing is why I believe much of our society, if they answered honestly, feel stuck. They will not look at their past or themselves and question the decisions they have made. They might never ask, "What part did I play?" This is why some of us remain a "victim" our entire lives. Unfortunately, many never heal, leaving them to live in dysfunction within a nagging loop of never-ending self-destructive behaviors.

The reality is we all have deep wounds and some of us have deep traumas, but if we can be brave enough to face them head on, then we can begin to heal.

There can often be a temporary retraumatization that takes place in order to fully process and heal old wounds. I am not going to say this is always the case, but I will say it has been the case for me. And it tends to get worse before it gets better depending on how dark and traumatic it was. But I have never felt stuck in my trauma because of all the emotional support in my life and my willingness to talk it out. You must find someone you feel comfortable with to speak openly with.

That's how you allow the pain to flow through you, so it can ultimately depart from your body.

At the very least, maintain an "irrational" faith in God to rescue you as I did when "digging up the past." My faith and belief in God have always been the fiercest when I have felt that I desperately needed him. It is my experience that the more you believe, the more you receive when it comes to your spiritual life.

Oftentimes that which is hysterical is historical. I have a friend who is grieving through the devastating loss of her teenage son. One of my neighbors recently lost her sister who was our age to cancer. Both cases call for hysterics and insurmountable waves of grief. In fact, any instance you feel grief, you need to release it, however it feels good to your body—whether it seems logical or not—through screaming, through tears, through holding your body and rocking back and forth. Let the grief leave.

What I have found in my own healing journey as an adult is when there is *not* life and death at play, but the emotions are uncontrolled, to ask myself, "When else have I felt this?" Let's get the best bang for our buck and consciously grieve what we believe we are upset about, but seek to see deeper while we are already triggered, and in the emotion, shall we?

A wound is what our body, our mind, and our hearts are left with when we experience physical or emotional pain. Until we process and heal our wounds, there will always be triggers that come up.

A trigger is simply an unhealed wound being pierced. But once you get to the root and heal that wound, it will slowly become a scar and no longer as sore to the touch. You don't have to experience intense triggers your entire life. It is my subjective opinion that the more scars, the more beautiful you are. I don't see them as rigid or rough to the touch when you pair them with a soft awareness. But you must keep your heart open to going back and revisiting them as often as you feel divinely led.

Healing is a miracle. It's spiritual.

Leave no experienced trigger to waste. They are our teachers and signs pointing us back home through healing our wounds to our whole and worthy selves. I have spent much of my adult life dodging triggers because of how awful they would make me feel, but as a self-taught, self-healer, I now welcome them and urge you to do the same. However, we should avoid placing ourselves in harm's way by staying in relationships with those who have been abusive and who have not sought help or developed the self-awareness required for change.

I believe in miracles and following the calls of your heart and soul to heal. Let me be your living proof of what is on the other side of healing until you can be your own.

Healing isn't for the faint of heart. Healing is for warriors.

I have studied Maslov's theory of basic needs for safety and belonging, and why when these are not met, we may feel traumatized, abandoned, or unsafe. When I was training to become a CASA (Court Appointed Special Advocate for Children) Volunteer, I was then introduced to the Adverse Childhood Experience (ACE) test that was developed by Dr. Vincent Felitti. This newfound knowledge and deeper awareness caused soulful grieving and healing as I further understood myself and felt seen.

I urge you to google "ACE test" or "ACE quiz" and take the very short quiz for yourself. You receive a score ranging from 0-10 based on the total number of questions you answer *yes* to. Did you know that the higher your score, the more likely you are to not only experiment with drugs, but become addicted? And the higher your score? The lower your life expectancy. Perhaps we are both fortunate to still be here.

We were instructed by the lady who trained us to complete the test. She said after we took it, to keep this in the back of our mind when evaluating the foster children who we would be advocating for—to help us understand them better. The higher their score, the more challenging they may be. What I know personally, the more difficult they are, the more love they need. She also suggested if we scored higher than a 6, then we might want to consider therapy for ourselves.

Personally, I scored an 8 out of 10. I have cheated death more times than I can count. Mental health professionals are not surprised at my childhood downfall. No wonder what was to come, came upon me. Although I was a "good girl," the granddaughter of a Southern Baptist Preacher, the teacher's pet, the annual winner of the DARE (Drug Abuse Resistance Education) essay contest, a straight-A student, and the kind of child every mother hoped her daughter would befriend because she "had her head on straight," a perfect storm mixed with a predisposition to mental illness was bound to unfold. And I was not built, supported, nor nourished to weather it. When the last straw came upon me, I would crumble.

I also want to invite you to study Internal Family Systems by Richard Schwartz that I mentioned in my note to you. If you do study it, I pray it will help you make even more sense of yourself like it did me.

The gist of IFS is this. We each have parts of ourselves that haven't healed, or subpersonalities, each with its own perspective and role. Oftentimes, when we encountered trauma as children, we disassociated in an unconscious effort to survive. But the clearest version of ourselves—the untriggered self—for me, the one writing this book, the one that is in flow and creativity with my children when we play after school, the one with the most compassionate nature who dreams up ideas to help others knowing we are all connected, the one who is open to explore all thoughts and feelings without judgment, the clarity and confidence that comes out when I speak on stage or in interviews sharing my story—you could call her my most ideal, healed, or highest self. She is the one that becomes more evident as my wounded parts further heal from being integrated and understood.

She is in me; she is in you, and she is inherently stronger and more resourceful than all our other wounded parts.

Ever find yourself, your husband, significant other, or friend throwing a tantrum? IFS teaches that there was something that happened at the age that a part of yours, his, or hers is manifesting that has not yet been healed—they could be there to protect us, to manage us, or put out fires. They are a part of our psyche borne out of a basic need to survive and take care of us. Personally, I have all kinds of ages that want to come out and have an opinion. What I say, as the clear and controlled adult to parent my inner children when they do, ranges from:

"I love you."

"I understand why this may feel hard for you."

"This is not fair, and you have every right to feel this way."

"You are going to get through this. You have me now."

"I'm sorry. I know how difficult this is for you."

And what I have learned to do before my speaking engagements where I share my story, is to have a compassionate chat with my inner "exiles" before speaking—this I have learned retraumatizes me less. It doesn't have to be out loud; it can be in my heart. But with my hand on my heart I communicate, "I know this is hard for you to hear. I know it makes you feel exposed and judged. I know you still feel so much shame. But we are safe now. The only way out of this to the freedom you seek is through it."

Straighten Your Crown Exercises:

- Explore your own childhood wounds, traumas, or ACE (adverse childhood experiences) by taking the test. Revisit a time when you felt like you didn't belong or felt unsafe.
- Consider the ways you are triggered today. What makes you panic or afraid or feel abandoned? Does it have something to do with the early trauma? Can you begin asking yourself, "When else have I felt this?"
- Write a letter to your inner child—thanking them for surviving and being brave. Soothe and be the parent or adult you wish you had when you were young.
- Stand in front of the adult version of yourself in a mirror, look at yourself in the eyes and read your letter aloud. Tell yourself, "I love you. You are safe. You are special. You are brave."
- Write down affirmations on Post-its and put them on mirrors all over your house, where you can remind yourself to repeat them aloud as you see them.

CHAPTER

Four

Finding Grace in Surrender After a Dark Night of the Soul

As agonizing as it was after winning the pageant, it was nowhere near the rock bottoms I had faced in my past. When I had quit drugs without any sort of emotional support or hospitalization, that was the most difficult. I was desperate for change, and it was by far my darkest day. And the time I was almost murdered by the man I loved? It felt like I had been thrown right back into the same bottomless pit after spending the past two years digging myself out. But the one good thing about rock bottom? It serves as a clean slate. For me, it was a fresh start on solid ground. This was the foundation on which I could begin to rebuild my life. And I did so, beautifully.

When it was time for my dark night of the soul over a decade later in 2021, I had the most favorable life circumstances with a world of love and support surrounding me. I believe a dark night is a God ordained season—a spiritual assignment—and an opportunity to evolve. It was time for my soul to finally get as free as she had ever been.

What came over me was a familiar feeling—where all my lies and feelings of unworthiness came crashing down on me. That is why I know God called me to pageants to help me heal as much as he led me to running and triathlons. One felt like an outlet for an endless release of repressed anger, aggression, and pain, while the other shined a light on all I still had left to recover and was the catalyst for my dark night.

My "dark night" lasted from August of 2021 until I began taking medication for my "major depressive disorder" in February of 2022. But in those short five months, I almost burned my life to the ground.

When my dark night of the soul came upon me, I had been married for three years to the most understanding and empathetic husband. Looking back on the divine order of things, I was set up and supported for life to get really messy. When it's the right person—and they're out there if finding someone is a dream of yours—they will have been forged by fire to have and to hold you if necessary. They can even help you heal. Their unconditional love will restore you in profound ways. I recommend *A Return to Love* by Marianne

Williamson and *Redeeming Love* by Francine Rivers while you wait.

When it comes to marriage or giving your heart to another person, it's one of the most important decisions you can make. Your partner can bring out the best in you. However, they can also bring out the worst. But there is always a still, small voice guiding you to the right path or person if you choose to listen closely. And when that voice gets loud, it's only because we ignored it for too long.

My husband and I met on Match.com. We kept the initial conversation brief, but immediately made plans for a date. From the very first day I met Dane in person, I intuitively felt safe to be seen. As I cried when I shared part of my story, he didn't run. This may have been because of the tragedies he had witnessed in his own life—losing one of three brothers, Ryan, by suicide the same month and year I wrote my first book, *Celia's Eyes*, and another, Tully, who is still living but whose life was stolen—perhaps, by his own traumas.

We are not aware of what would have possessed his baby brother to smoke marijuana at nine years old. This is recognized as an unfavorable mix with a genetic tendency for schizophrenia which Tully apparently had. Today, he resides in a group home funded by the state of Tennessee. My husband feels guilty for not telling his parents when he first found the drugs over thirty years ago. But he was only a little boy, too.

On our second date, Dane and I enjoyed dinner before heading back to his place for drinks. While chatting in his kitchen, he had shared with me the fate of both brothers. I claimed if God could save me, he could bring back Tully. I innocently believed then, and still do, that if I could be rescued from where I had been and completely transform my life, then *anyone* can.

It was that same childlike faith that has always supported me and continues to do so.

My husband has seen and understood me to my core from the very beginning. For this reason, he has supported every move I've made to share my story and help others when many other men wouldn't. After sharing his family's history with me in his kitchen, he told me that I was the strongest person he had ever met. It wasn't only his words that brought me to believe him. It was because of all the trauma he and his family had endured; how could he *not* know strength?

He was forged by the fires in his own life and as a result, our hearts were perfectly aligned.

He was built to see me through the dark night of my soul—when all the lies I had told myself to not feel the pain I had been avoiding since childhood came crashing and crushing down—on us both. The truth is, we almost didn't survive it.

We had only been dating for six months when I became pregnant with the boys. Well, we thought it was only one at first. The night I shared that I had taken a positive pregnancy test, I realized I was finally seeing the dream I had held since I was a little girl playing with her dolls. He wasn't nearly as excited as I was at first. His initial reaction was, "You know we aren't going to get married just because you're pregnant, right?" I said I understood. I tried to play it cool. But I was ecstatic about the idea of becoming the mother of *his* child.

Before we had our first ultrasound, I had been studying example images online so I could understand what I would be looking at. When my doctor asked, "Wow, can you guess what we see here?"

As Dane later admitted, he wanted to shush me and just allow the doctor to do her job when I had proudly exclaimed, "Twins!"

By the time we made it to the parking garage, Dane was noticeably enthusiastic and into the pregnancy as much as I was. Seeing them made it more real for him. Apparently, he had always wanted to have twins since he was a child, so we were living out one of his dreams too. He playfully teased, "Can we start telling people I have super sperm now?"

As we got further along in my pregnancy, my insecurities grew deeper. I could no longer pretend. Under the direction of my therapist, I had to tell him that I wanted marriage. She taught me that my feeling as though I needed it—that didn't make me wrong.

When I shared the conversation I had with my therapist, Dane told me he was always going to marry me. And that he would personally rather wait, but if it meant something to me, then he would of course do whatever it took to please me.

A few months later and a week or so before Christmas, he officially proposed. We said "I do" on January 17th of 2019, two months before our twin boys were born. I always joke that my pageants are my version of a wedding (including the cost) since I never had one. We had married on a Thursday morning and had our teeth cleaned at the dentist that afternoon—so romantic. I think I always struggled with a little guilt and questioned his love for me since I felt like it was forced out of my need to be a married woman the day I gave birth to my children. I know I had pressured him.

After winning Mrs. Tennessee in August, I had to prepare for the national competition in Las Vegas which was a mere eleven weeks away that November. I was under a lot of stress. I was also having a nervous breakdown—which for a woman like you and I—that ultimately means a breakthrough.

During the months of August to February, I numbed the feelings of cognitive dissonance by drinking heavily—more heavily than usual. This led to a night in October where I put myself in a vulnerable position. Even with my family's hotel villa directly in sight, I went too far emotionally in a conversation with another man. We were in a group setting, but somehow still managed to cross the line and bond over our traumas. I never saw him again, but found comfort in the conversation that did not end that night—his attention feeding a wounded part and her need to escape from reality. By the time I got to the national pageant in November, I was proving my thoughts to be right.

They don't really know me. I am unworthy. I don't deserve to be here.

It's called a self-fulfilling prophecy. This concept refers to the tendency for people to act in ways that confirm their beliefs about themselves. The beliefs we hold shape our behavior, leading to consequences from our actions that confirm it. If you believe you are unworthy, you will unconsciously create situations or respond to them in a manner that will result in negative outcomes that only reinforce that belief.

Our thoughts are powerful. They can become beliefs which beget feelings. Our feelings of unworthiness only lead to a cycle of negative experiences. That is why it is so important for us to heal our limiting beliefs and guard our thoughts as they dictate our lives. But we can't do that without healing the trauma from which they originated. I will repeat.

The trauma happened to you first. Negative beliefs about yourself emerged. The actions followed.

A reigning Mrs. Tennessee competing for a national title should be in love with her husband, not with one foot out the door. I was a phony. And I knew it. All I wanted to do at the peak of my life thus far on the outside was to run away.

When I arrived in Vegas, I was to be there for ten days—the first day being completely unsupervised and unattended. Some of the girls that I knew had asked me to go shopping with them and explore the city, but I couldn't be a friend at this time. I had so much shame and such a dirty secret I could not share with anyone. It was eating me alive.

I walked around the city and had lunch at a Mexican restaurant where I had consumed way too many margaritas. Drunk, I got up the nerve to ask the server where I could buy "weed" because I knew it had become legal there. When she pointed directly across the street, in my altered state, I felt I was in Heaven.

I spent a few hundred dollars on pens, gummies, and enough oil that I thought would last me forever. I hadn't been high since the first few weeks I was dating my husband three and a half years prior. That was a record since I first became a "stoner" at fifteen years old after the sexual abuse. The drugs took to me then.

Dane had told me when we first started dating that he didn't mind if I indulged, provided that, it wasn't "all the time." Well, I once smoked every day. I felt like a few times a week was an improvement. He quickly realized this and laid down the law. Because Dane was the whole package and everything I had ever dreamed of in a guy, it made it easy to quit—*for him*—at the time.

Fast forward to being by myself, drunk, in the middle of a nervous breakdown soon to be breakthrough? I think we could have all seen this coming.

A week prior to me leaving for my national pageant in Vegas, I met an old friend and shared my shameful secret with her. We had a couple glasses of wine, and because I was anxious and back in runaway mode, I made the mistake of taking a drag off her cigarette pen. I was instantly addicted. I drove straight to a gas station on my way home where I bought two of my own which I snuck in my suitcase to Vegas.

Now I had weed pens, gummies, and vape pens to add to my suitcase of dishonorable secrets. Add in the pressure of attempting to convince the judges: *Pick me, I am your model wife and human.* Talk about confronting an identity crisis.

Dane had flown up right before the preliminary and finals competition. Our fights had gotten so bad that I had my dad lined up as a Plan B in case he didn't fly in to escort me. It was always a threat that he wouldn't come, but Dane said it was never true. And I believe him.

Right before showtime, I asked my husband to grab something I needed from my luggage and run it to the room where I was having my hair and makeup done. As he searched through my suitcase, he discovered all my contraband. But, in steadfast Dane fashion, he didn't say a word as to not affect or hinder my performance that night.

Once again, I successfully fooled the judges. I placed Top 15 in my second pageant, and my first national one. I should have been proud of my accomplishment, but nothing would have satisfied me, not even winning. It felt like rejection, and that was the final nail in my coffin. The evening after the pageant, we got real.

Honestly, it felt like a relief for him to find out about *almost* everything. Because those secrets were consuming me from within. Much to my surprise, he didn't plan to leave me. That made me feel something I needed from him because I had always felt like the darker parts of myself were not worthy or deserving of being accepted, much less, *loved* by myself—and especially not by a man who had never even experimented with drugs. But he proved day in and day out of that dark night that he loved me unconditionally. He could tell I was struggling, and his goal was to see me through it. Before I left Vegas, I finished off my cigarette pen and vowed to never buy another. And I didn't. By then, I was an avid runner and triathlete, for goodness' sake. I knew it would bring me down fast.

The Monday after the national pageant while we were eating dinner (and me drinking) at our local country club with the boys, I surrendered to my fate and blurted out my dirtiest secret. I did it on purpose in public because I feared his reaction. I was exhausted from the lies, and the marijuana only made me more tired and depressed. I didn't know how to solve the problem. But I couldn't continue hiding it from him.

So, when I say my dark night of the soul came crushing down on us both, this is why. It wasn't until our darkest days that I finally believed Dane loved me and that he genuinely *chose* me. Looking back, through my actions rooted in my limiting beliefs about myself, I was driving us to this very moment where he would leave me. This was his out—his pass to abandon me. But he would not. His actions told me in a way I could finally believe and see what I needed to hear and hold onto for the rest of our lives together, *I choose you.*

In January of 2022, I was going to be seeing my coworker again for another event. I felt that it was too soon after I confided in my husband about the emotional affair, bringing that darkness and deceit to light. I felt emotionally disconnected from my marriage, while my husband remained the glue that held us together. I even spent eight thousand dollars on a three-month lease for an apartment where I never stayed a single night or moved in any belongings. I suppose it can't be considered wasted if you achieved your goal. I was in the wrong overall and I know this, but we both had our issues to work through. We still do. We all do.

Although it felt like my heart was no longer in my marriage, we both wanted it to be.

To break free from any addiction, I have learned that you must control your environment until you can control yourself. I felt terrified to see my coworker again. My mental health suffered any time we interacted. With my darkest days behind me, I feared being sucked back in to what was toxic to my spirit, and I am sure his too. As with every life and death moment throughout my existence, on a cold winter day, I prayed for a miracle, and I received one.

Deep down, I did not want to break up my family, and worse, me be the cause. I obviously still loved Dane. I wanted better for everyone, especially my two boys who I had dreamed of giving them a better life than I had. So as my husband embraced me and begged the part of my heart who had checked out of our marriage to come back to him while I was in the middle of packing for my work trip, for the first time since everything unfolded, I prayed that familiar silent prayer to God, *Help me.*

The very next morning we woke up to find that we were snowed and iced in. I had no idea paralyzing weather was going to hit us. My SUV couldn't even get down my driveway, much less, drive three and a half hours to Memphis. This created even more distance until—just like with the drugs, I could feel free of that which was poisonous to my soul. Call it coincidence. I call it an act of God. Because in my reality, it was the miracle I had prayed for and the sign I needed to see he was going to help me. Help *us*.

We survived that which could have killed us as a couple. Given my awareness that a divorce would have perpetuated the same trauma I had experienced onto my own children, it really was a matter of life and death for my soul.

Not every moment has been easy since. We are two wounded souls, having a human experience as is everyone else. But this was our rock bottom—and as I have said, a positive aspect about them is they are solid ground—and that solid ground was the basis of which we could begin to rebuild our marriage. We were tested, and we proved that we will never allow darkness to drive us apart.

There is a strength that is born within us and in our relationships when we face and overcome adversity—a quiet confidence. A feeling that, "Come what may, but you won't break us. If that didn't kill us, nothing will."

Don't think I would change a thing, although there is always a price to pay. Because of the pressure I put on my husband to marry me, I lived with feeling like my husband didn't genuinely want to be with me whether it was true or not. The venomous emotional affair nearly swallowed us whole. The dark night was shrouded in darkness and filled with despair, but at least I emerged from it never again questioning my husband's love for me. In the case of my path, things have played out and run their wild course. I believe my husband would agree that although we would never go back to our darkest days, we have come out on the other side stronger for it.

The last day I drank so much as a sip of alcohol was in July of 2022. I don't have the date memorized because I wasn't even sure that would be the last time. But one day turned into two, and then one month turned into a year. By now, I am so far removed I would never jeopardize my peace. For the sober curious, you may fear it's too valuable to eliminate from your life like I once did, but from my experience, my relationships have become by far, much richer.

It took me to the day I had my last drink of alcohol to finally set aside marijuana, in any form. I know that it made me more anxious overall, but in the moment—the first few if nothing else, I always felt a relief. But I yearned for a life beyond the confines of my longing to flee.

I wanted to be free—a recurring dream.

I give credit to the SNRI medication I took from February of 2022 until September of 2023 for helping to make things easier to feel for a season. I knew I needed it. But the moment Dane agreed with me on how essential medication would be for me was the day a fight drove me to spend eight thousand dollars for that three-month lease. After being on medication for my "major depressive disorder" for five months, I finally felt calm enough to make rational decisions, such as, you know, "This does not serve me. And in fact, it never has. So why am I doing it?" Alcohol or marijuana never helped me achieve lasting peace or satisfaction. But when you are in so much psychic pain, you don't ask yourself these questions.

Although never diagnosed, I was the classic textbook definition of borderline personality disorder in relationships. The BPD symptoms never allowed me to get too close to the opposite and feel at ease. My fears of abandonment made it feel painful to even have a text conversation with a guy, let alone date. But when I met my husband, his life experiences had shaped him, had forged him, were predestined to bring him to the day he would meet me and be up for the challenge of "loving me until all the holes in my heart would be filled." That is what he promised to do in that same kitchen. And he did. He has. And continues to do so.

I would experience anxiety anytime I would get close to a man I cared about and then perceived their distance. There just isn't a medication to treat someone who has irrational fears of people leaving them. There is no treatment to stop one from self-sabotaging their relationship because they don't trust they are loved and, in their delusion, go from thinking someone is their hero to one day cruel. There is no remedy to make someone not feel anxious when waiting for a text reply from the opposite sex unless they take a Xanax every time they send one.

I was originally prescribed Xanax for the anxiety and panic I experienced during a breakup in 2015. They supported me during a difficult period and didn't take me down a troubled path. I never even got a refill. But when I broke off another relationship, just before Dane had come into my life three years later, I had gotten a new prescription. I had traveled to a dark place this time—one of dependency—and had barely brought myself back out weeks before we met.

Knowing I was abusing them, Dane pulled the plug on me using Xanax even for my panic attacks when he would travel for work with other women which felt like torture. Although they were prescribed to me to ease the anxiety, true to my addictive nature, once they kicked in and I felt good, I would take more than the suggested dose. Benzodiazepines are known to be very addictive. Dane was also triggered by them specifically because his brother, Ryan, was under the influence of benzodiazepines when he ended his life in 2011.

It is a miracle that I have been unmedicated since September of 2023. I weaned off under the care of my nurse practitioner who had supported this dream of mine. Medication helped me become completely sober. There, I was forced to face my pain. There was no more running. The SNRI medication helped to provide a buffer which eased the ache and allowed me to go deeper than I ever had when confronting my childhood trauma. Through the healing and processing of my sexual abuse, specifically, the labels of major depressive disorder and borderline personality disorder left me. For me, my mental illnesses were merely symptoms of unhealed trauma. Because once I worked through the trauma, the symptoms I exhibited of these disorders miraculously resolved themselves. And I am not the only one. I recommend *Lost Connections* by Johann Hari of you'd like to hear more success stories.

As a child, I rarely felt safe. The actions of the adults in my life told me I was "not enough" for them to be there for me and meet my needs. So as a result, growing up, I became a people-pleasing, perfectionist who would do anything to gain friends' and teachers' favor. The overachieving is driven from a part within me that doesn't feel she is quite "enough." I will not lie to myself, or you, and pretend I have no room to grow. Rather, I face it. I bring it to light. And then I heal. Nobody is perfect.

When I was twelve years old, my mother attended a Benny Hinn event hoping for a miracle for one of my younger siblings, as she was concerned about their sexual orientation. During his miracle crusade, she was "touched by God." Her experience had triggered what psychologists would call a manic episode and researchers in the fields of spirituality and consciousness might call a kundalini awakening by the way she described what happened to her.

With her hands lifted in worship to God, she sensed a surge of electricity flow through her veins, radiating from her hands, which trembled for months afterwards. She became an instant fanatic. Her erratic behavior was the catalyst for her separation from my stepdad.

YOU ARE A QUEEN

When they officially dissolved their marriage, my mother moved us constantly from home to home, but she would never move us out of the small town that ridiculed her and made us both feel like outcasts everywhere we turned after her encounter with "God." His leaving and us never exchanging words triggered my abandonment wound. But becoming an outcast in a town where I was once adored by the people in my church, the teachers at my school, and the friends I grew up with–this was the trauma that was the root of my depression and my endless quest for belonging.

An ex-boyfriend of mine at thirteen years old told our friends he wouldn't go back out with me after I broke up with him because "her mom throws up demons in a trash can," which wasn't a lie. My stepdad told the whole small town about her strange and unpredictable behavior during their divorce. I suppose she was finding her freedom in her own way, but I had no stable port to weather a storm of that magnitude.

I didn't initially turn my back on God. But when my mother and "God's" madness uprooted me from a house I grew up in where all my trophies, report cards, and story writing contests I had won in school stayed because no one had packed my things for me—and I was separated from my little brother and sister I had grown up with—a cloud of darkness came over me so thick, I remember dreaming of being taken to Heaven as early as thirteen years old. I prayed to Jesus to please hurry up and come back. Eventually resentment set in for both my mother and her God, which I mistakenly believed was the one I grew up loving.

She made me attend church every night of the week during her manic phase—chasing down her highs from one revival to the next. It wasn't a balanced way of living, and I hated every minute of it. She couldn't make her husband, or my other siblings come with us because they were his too, but she had full power to impose what seemed like her madness upon me.

There was a lot of what her churches liked to call "deliverance" going on. I saw demons cast out of people, and I saw them manifest in bizarre ways because I was told they like to "show out" when there was an audience. Even more troubling, she was visiting these churches nightly to have them exercised and cast out of her in my presence. The insanity was only intensifying.

I saw blood vessels popping out of more than one family member as they screamed bloody murder. While restrained, they kicked and roared before one of their "murder" demons I was told finally left. I couldn't finish watching. I buried my head because I was afraid. I was exposed to my mother throwing up demons constantly, not just at church. She would place a strainer in the trash can so she could "see" them. Beginning at age twelve, this had become my reality. There were even two occasions where she only consumed water for forty days as she fasted. Both times, she appeared to be dying, but it wasn't until her second 40 day fast that was she hospitalized. Experiencing my mother go through her own nightmare was traumatic.

One weekday evening around midnight, I was forced to have strangers pray for me during a revival. As they placed their hands on my head, in a fit of rage, I announced I was done with God. I told the God I believed in to "GO AWAY" in my heart as mean, true, and as heartfelt as I possibly could. I was wearing a pink, ribbed, mock turtleneck sweater as I stared down at the seat of the cream-colored pew. I meant it with all my heart; although I had no idea where turning my back on my faith would lead my life.

If God could take my mother and stable childhood away from me and replace it with chaos and a seemingly insane person, I wanted no part of that kind of God. She exposed me to all sorts of unseemly characters and situations that a child should never be around. One of these people, her employee and a member of the church where I told God to "GO AWAY," sexually assaulted me when I was barely fifteen years old. A part of my soul detached to shield my mind from further pain. I disassociated. In many ways I would remain stuck at fifteen years old until I healed this wound. I learned twenty years later that this was the root of all my self-hatred when I was finally ready to see it for what it was, abuse.

At the time of the assault, I had no idea how to cope. I was a child, after all, and the assailant was a child predator. What was worse, is that after I told my mother, she did nothing to prevent him from approaching me again. She made me feel responsible because she truly believed I was "partly" to blame because of how I dressed (in clothes she bought me) and because *I* knew he was married. His wife worked at the furniture store as well.

I never shared this with my dad who could have intervened because I was so ashamed until I was thirty-seven old. I couldn't even "look at it" when Dane read my first book while we were dating. In *Celia's Eyes*, I explained the assault in detail and took more accountability than a child ever should while he called it what it was. He said, "Celia, you were molested. And what your mother did was wrong." But I couldn't fully process this news at the time. I wasn't ready to face the fact that my mother would hire someone back to work for her that molested me. I wasn't ready to see that she didn't love me enough to advocate for me, her own daughter, by going to the police. I wasn't ready to feel the grief and ultimately the relief from processing the root of so much pain. I wasn't ready to acknowledge the deep pain and call it what it was. Sexual abuse was the kind of trauma that would take more than a grandma drawing candles on a cake to distract me from.

Within two months of the assault, before drugs or alcohol, I began to cut myself, just to feel something. When that stopped working, I smoked marijuana. Again, I wanted to feel something—anything. A cutter has an identity. So does the bad girl. I understand them both. I had been so numb and frozen by the trauma, drugs felt like the only alternative.

As a teenager, I truly thought I was doing myself a favor. I walked into the role of a "scapegoat" in psychology terms. A scapegoat is the one in a family who is unjustly blamed for problems or negative outcomes, which diverts attention or responsibility from the actual source of the issue. I was already being blamed for being molested. *My* crazy, I would make sure, exceeded all the other crazy around me so I wouldn't hurt anymore. *I became the issue.* No one had to face themselves for years because their time was spent praying my life would be saved.

As far as my reputation in my small town was concerned, I was already an outcast. No one respectable would want to date me because of my mother. What did I feel I had to lose by going down this path?

Many people assume there is something wrong with individuals who become addicts; however, I believe it's usually their circumstances that drive them to seek out drugs to feel better in the first place. The body really does keep the score of our traumas and all addictions are our body's way of righting itself from the pain we've endured. I suggest reading *The Body Keeps the Score* by Dr. Bessel van der Kolk for a deeper understanding.

Like so many drug addicts, I didn't realize that my trauma had led me there. I just felt terrible about myself. I felt like there was something fundamentally wrong with me.

I considered myself defective. My life was spinning out of control.

One day, after a week of not showering or being able to leave my bed, I felt lower than I had ever been. At that moment, I surprised myself when I began to plead to the only person I felt could save me, Jesus—the same one who I had told I wanted nothing to do with just a few years earlier. I asked him to *help me*. For the first time in years, in the fetal position of the darkest, bleakest, most lonely moment of my life, I reached out and asked him to rescue me. I surrendered myself completely to him. By silently praying two of the most powerful words in the English language, "*Help me,*" I was able to see the tiniest crack of light open for me in the darkness. This was my rock-bottom moment. This was the day I surrendered. This is why you must not enable another. I look and see my rock bottom as a gift.

I didn't heal overnight. I didn't magically become the sober woman I am today—or ever become a saint. In fact, I didn't even begin to feel worthy—for years—not until after my dark night of the soul I shared with you. But it was enough to get me started on the journey toward the light. I was able to take the first steps—to shower, change my clothes, and admit, I couldn't do this on my own.

I asked for grace. As a child I was fully versed in the Bible. During Sunday school and worship services at church, I had heard of a thing called grace—the spontaneous and unmerited gift from God that saves us from our sins, sanctifies us, and sets us free. With grace, I was told, anything was possible. *I was possible.* I could do anything. I wanted to be free from the pain and the drugs that I was desperately drawn to but was fully aware were going to kill me if I didn't stop. Above all, I yearned to escape my profound feelings of unworthiness and disgust in myself for the actions I took in search of feeling alive— particularly those that placed me in more danger and harm's way. Ultimately, I wanted to be purified, sanctified, and made whole—what the Christians I grew up with called, "Holy."

The reality is most of us want to feel *whole*, inhabit ourselves fully, and not be afraid to feel—the good and the bad. I desired to feel that way too. I wanted grace to wash over me. But the only way to do that was to surrender and ask for help first. And again, that was only the first step on my journey, my very long journey back home to myself.

Straighten Your Crown Exercises:

- Remember or consider your own dark nights of the soul—when you felt alone in the dark or trapped in a seemingly hopeless predicament with no apparent escape.
- Consider what brought you there. What "situation" or "experience" seemed to be the catalyst for you? For me, it was a series of traumas punctuated by a major one, that left me incapable of coping in the

ways I always had (as a perfectionist) and seeking relief in cutting, then drugs.

- Consider the ways you currently seek "relief"—and identify which ones seem to be sanctioned by society (workaholism, drinking wine with friends, shopping, overexercising, binging Netflix, obsessing over one's appearances, etc.) and which ones are deemed "addictions" (drugs, alcohol, sex, gambling, etc.)
- Examine whether you feel you are in control of the situation, or if you feel like you are no longer capable of changing your behavior on your own.
- Write or pray a plea for help. Consider what areas you are willing to hand over to God, Jesus, or the Higher Being of your choice. This spiritual path is personal.
- Consider what your life would be like if you felt whole, experienced grace, and could be magically transformed overnight.

CHAPTER

Five

Patience Is a Virtue

No one crawls their way out of rock bottom and immediately has it all figured out. It takes time—a lot of time—and patience. In fact, one of the most important virtues for any Queen is patience. As much as I have known that I needed to be patient with myself, I am not saying it has always been easy or that I have passed every test.

There is an old saying that you will keep experiencing the same lesson over and over until you have learned what it is meant to teach you. Patience is just one of the many lessons I have had to learn the hard way. But sometimes the most trying experiences are designed to teach us exactly what we need most.

Patience is something I needed to work on, and it took a lot of it to get through those tough years and find my way to the other side. The deeper I heal, I find that being patient comes to me more naturally. You know you have mastered the art of patience when you feel a wave of peace while you wait.

Like so many others who are climbing out of their rock bottom and feeling their way through the darkness as they struggle toward the light, I grabbed hold of the wrong things as I was trying to make my way out. Giving myself grace as I type this, but the truth is my delays have been due to my impatience and trying to take matters into my own hands. Please learn from my mistakes—and find your peace and pray for patience.

You must begin with a dream—a desperate want for more out of the life you're living. Finding a compassionate community to surround yourself with makes healing feel possible. It was through my faith, the power of prayer, and my church community, that I broke completely free from my drug addiction, smoking marijuana, getting drunk, and any relationship that made me feel taken advantage of at the age of twenty.

I was making friends at church and beginning to regain my strength. But my void was quite large after quitting drugs cold turkey, and I still didn't feel whole. How could I? Not only did I have the pain that made me turn to drugs in the first place, but now the physical and psychological trauma from doing them. I was eight months clean from hard drugs and four months free from all other entanglements—relationships that made me feel used, getting drunk, and marijuana—when a man close to my age, and who I found attractive, walked into the bar where I was working during lunch one afternoon. He was on "intensive probation" for assaulting cops while drunk, but his family business that he had part owned was within walking distance from where I worked. This made it easy for him to venture out.

Since humans can help ease the ache of loneliness, naturally, I felt drawn to him. But it was my lack of patience paired with a giant hole in my heart that latched on to the first relationship that came my way. I found solace in this other person, who I thought understood me, only to find myself once again trapped in a new version of hell—an abusive relationship. I tried to escape, but couldn't stay away, caught up in a different, though no less familiar addictive cycle, a codependent and toxic relationship.

Just like the drugs, I used the relationship to feel whole, but I never quite was able to. The same emptiness—and what I know now to be unhealed trauma—that drove me to the drugs, drove me to him. I couldn't escape the void because it wasn't something outside of me that I needed to heal me—healing had to come from within.

I had met a person who I could feel a connection with since he was an alcoholic and survivor of childhood trauma. We both knew what it felt like to be misunderstood. I thought we were the same, but we weren't the same at all. At only twenty years old, I married a man after knowing him for three weeks that turned out to be violent and abusive. After the brazen escape for my life, I set myself free and received an annulment eight months later.

By the time I had turned twenty-one, I had kicked hard drugs, married, had it annulled, and managed to survive an abusive spouse. It took years for me to fully trust myself to make sound decisions about who I should choose to have in my life. Trusting yourself is crucial to living your life whole. But there was just no way, and for good reason, I would be able to do that any time soon. For the next four years, I not only released myself to *my* Higher Power, Jesus, but I read hundreds of self-help books to figure out where I went wrong and how to get better. I had even begun seeing a counselor for the very first time in my life. The question I would one day ask myself would be, "But did I really go wrong on my own? Or was it the emptiness from my childhood that fueled the fire within?"

From what I had read and learned through therapy, I realized I had formed a trauma bond with my ex. Trauma bonding refers to the strong emotional attachment that can develop between individuals who have shared traumatic experiences, particularly in abusive or harmful relationships. This bond often forms when one person experiences intense emotional or physical distress, and the other person alternates between providing comfort and causing harm. The cycle of abuse and subsequent reconciliation creates a powerful, although unhealthy, connection that can make it difficult for the victim to leave the relationship. Trauma bonding can lead to feelings of loyalty, dependence, and confusion, as the victim may struggle to reconcile the love and care they receive with the pain and fear of abusive behavior. These relationships can feel addictive. And that is why leaving them is just as difficult as quitting hard drugs.

I also still had an enormous amount of shame associated with sex, because of the molestation I had experienced and the promiscuity that followed. Because of my religious upbringing and the psychic pain I would experience from simply getting emotionally close to the opposite sex—coupled with my grit and a determination to break the cycle of trauma and shame that led to these dark paths—it was the easiest decision to become celibate. It was my only choice. I knew I couldn't be with another person until I had given my mind, body, and soul the time they needed to heal.

I had a multitude of girlfriends during this stage of my life. My life was full of color despite being celibate. My calendar was filled with lunch dates, movie dates, and dinner dates—with my girls. Most of my girlfriends were older. Some were the age I am writing you today.

I needed these women for a few reasons—they soothed what is called the "mother wound" in psychology. The mother wound refers to the emotional, psychological, and relational impact that the bond or lack thereof with our mothers can have on our lives. The older women, specifically, were very nurturing. Their attention and encouraging nature helped me fill the unmet emotional needs that I had craved from my mother as a child.

Each of my girlfriends were humans I could feel safe to be around as I healed. They helped me co-regulate. Co-regulation doesn't necessarily mean you discuss or process a trauma with someone else—you can, but you can also benefit from the social connections as they aid in calming your nervous system. Simply being in someone else's presence who you feel secure with can help you.

One of these girlfriends tried to set me up with a friend of her husband's, but I found fault with every man. There was no one who met my standards. As she and I got closer, I shared more details from my past, and then she understood. I had created a lengthy checklist to fool proof my poor judgment in men. I know I had appeared too strict and serious for a twenty-five-year-old, but it worked out well for me in the end. Afterall, I had written my first book at twenty-five years old with this mind before my time.

I had been celibate for years when I wrote my first book—where I purged and cleared out everything dark inside of me. And when I say everything, I mean every dark thing, As I had mentioned previously, writing it had healed me in profound ways. But did you know that I had written the first version of *Celia's Eyes* in three days?

On the final night of my writing binge, an irrational fear that had been haunting and paralyzing me since I was a little girl had come over me while I was wrapping up. Scared stiff,

I shut my computer and ran to my mother's room where I was still living. In a voice that didn't sound like my own, I begged, "Mommy, mommy, please hold me."

I believe a dark entity that had been with me since I was a child was manifesting before it had finally left me. I have had nearly fourteen years to change my mind about this. As I have shared with you, I was forced to watch demons exercised as a child. I know *for a fact* there are other realms. What I experienced from the walk to my mother's bedroom, to her holding me like a baby, to needing to use the bathroom, then fainting on the way there—none of that was of this world—and who better to have that experience around than her? She is one of the few people who would understand.

I believe it was a spirit of fear. Maybe it had come on me when I would watch scary movies with my stepdad as a child? I was taught that could happen, but I have had a lot of insane influences in my life. I always say take what feels true to you and leave the rest. And that happens to resonate for me.

I originate mortgages for a living. I don't have any interest in obsessing over or studying dark entities. But that is my best guess. It even had its own voice—that of a child that wasn't one of mine. For all my mother had seen when it had come to her own demons, she was unphased.

When the writing binge had ended that Sunday, every inch of my face was covered with cystic acne, as if I was a meth addict again. When I first began using meth at eighteen, my skin immediately broke out. My cystic acne had become so severe while doing it. At a certain point, your teeth could decay and fall out as well. You will also see meth addicts with scabs all over from picking at their skin.

I want you to see that it's been a struggle to get where I am today. The drugs made me ugly on the inside and the outside. As much as I have needed patience as I heal my inner world, I have had to have patience as I healed my appearance.

I had two skin treatments in my early 20's on my face to help with the scarring—one before I wrote my first book, and the other after. During both, I was put to sleep under anesthesia and sent home the same day. It was with a fractional CO_2 laser. I couldn't be seen in public for a week. This as well as microneedling in my 30's has helped my scarring and the texture of my skin tremendously.

The same medical doctor who had performed the procedure on my face had told me that I would struggle with cystic acne for the rest of my life because the crystals from the meth would be trapped under my skin and continue to surface at any moment's notice. I was five years clean, and they were still coming up occasionally. I have not researched his theory to be backed by science, but it makes sense to me. They would be painful to the touch, round, and quite large. And because of my lack of patience, I would pick at them which didn't help their appearance.

After the "door incident"—that was the "weapon" my "husband" first assaulted me with the evening I had to "Go now" and make an escape for my own life, I was left with another scar. To this day, my right eye won't open as large as my left. There is a protrusion that only I may notice.

The scars that remain on my face today are a reminder that no matter how much I have transformed, my past will always be a part of me. I know I lived through it to help others. My imperfections serve as a reminder to never forget where I have come from—not from a shameful place—but from a place of humility.

I also know what it's like to have to get a third job to add to your full time and existing part time server job to pay back the hospital for a bill you received from being beaten by your husband. I know what it's like to not order extra cheese because of the cost. I know what it's like to be on food stamps. There was a time I needed them. Life has humbled me, and I see it as a gift.

It is my belief that God purged me of all the darkness trapped inside of me the weekend I wrote my first book. I needed a miracle and a kickstart to my healing. The irrational fears, the paranoia when left home alone as a recovering drug addict, plus all the toxins from the meth I had ingested that I was told would be resurfacing for the rest of my life—they all left me that weekend. I have never experienced cystic acne since. And that fear that manifested? It made me faint before I got sick in the bathroom, and it finally left me. It has never attacked me again—the same fear I grew up with that my first therapist said, "You're not crazy. Children have wild imaginations," when I told him about how it would haunt and paralyze me as a child and questioning if that was "normal."

Within weeks of writing my first book, I was well enough to know I needed to move out of my mom's house. Shortly after being out on my own, God revealed to me that she wasn't mentally well. I was not able to see this as a child. But I began processing that trauma in that moment. I know that she understood things that others didn't spiritually, but the mania and obsession with demons reflected her mental illness. My hometown may have been wrong in how they treated us, but they were not wrong in saying that something wasn't right.

It was a spiritual experience for me to write down all that I had been through and survived. In the process of writing, I felt I had been given a vision of the future. However, I had to become the woman I had envisioned if I wanted to fulfill that future.

To become her, I had to heal her.

From then until now, that's exactly what I have been doing. Even the years when I had buried my book and had been avoiding my healing—they were productive in their own right. I established my mortgage business during that period. God doesn't waste *anything*. There is no wrong path to get here. Three steps forward and two steps back still equates to one step ahead. It's been a long road of becoming for me. But that's exactly what I did. I finally became who I always wanted to be.

It demands time and requires patience for your mind, body, and soul to heal, and that's why it's so important you give yourself permission to pause, step away, and reflect. My life has been a quest of going deeper and deeper to seek the answers only I had. It was as though my soul was seeking its way home.

Straighten Your Crown Exercises:

- Get real about your past choices and current behaviors.
- Create a vision of your "Highest Self" so you can see yourself as the Queen you really are.
- Devise a plan to become this version of yourself by asking what you need to do to achieve that.
- Consider removing behaviors, relationships, and activities from your life that may be holding you back. (i.e., I changed my phone number, stopped hanging out with the same people, and no longer dated/had sex for a period.)
- Write down and/or tell your own story—purging everything you've been through. Pretend you have an audience who needs to hear what you have to say.
- Make amends with people you have harmed, remembering this takes time too and not everyone will be ready to forgive you or trust you right away.

- Make a list of standards for yourself—things you are willing to wait for. (I set extremely high standards for myself and others.)
- Explore various faiths if you feel you have lost yours—or if you feel content in your own faith, you can go deeper, and surrender.

CHAPTER

Six

A Queen Forgives Herself—Making Peace with Your Shadow Self

For years, I held myself responsible for what had happened to me as a child. I blamed the molestation by an adult on the clothes I wore. I felt my addiction was solely my fault. I was embarrassed for not feeling strong enough to leave an abusive relationship. There is no shortage of things that we, as women, can beat ourselves up over.

In June of 2005, I had fallen back for what I can now say was my final time. I was doing my best to leave the hard drugs behind and had been making great strides. But one afternoon, I started taking Xanax, smoking marijuana, and drinking alcohol with a friend. By the end of the night, I had taken nine, blue football-shaped Xanax. That was eighteen times the amount I was ever prescribed for actual panic attacks. Under this influence, I made the poor decision to buy cocaine. I was so out of my mind that I had even called my dad's home line and left a voicemail at 3 am out of nowhere as I hadn't spoken to him regularly or seen him in five years.

When the cocaine had run out, the only drug available to me was crack cocaine. You're familiar with the narrative; I gave it a shot. Between the crack and the combination of the other drugs, I was crazed. While the first bit of crack was given to me for free, when I felt I needed more, it cost money that I didn't have.

A few days later, I was still lying in bed so depressed over how I had agreed to let my body be used by a dealer to obtain more drugs. My guy "friend" called him in the early hours while he was asleep to bring me more crack cocaine. I was incapacitated. I wouldn't have even been able to write my name in that state. I had been vomiting off and on as I always did during my coke binges. While I fully acknowledge my role in the circumstances that I found myself in, by definition, I was a victim of rape. Any individual consenting to engage in sexual activity must be of legal age *and* sound mind to make that decision. It's a gray area where two people are intoxicated. But this dealer was clear headed and sober while I was not. That's what makes it so wrong.

I had never flashed anyone when offered more drugs to do so. When I was eighteen, I turned down five hundred dollars to strip on a table at a party, money I could have used to buy more cocaine. None of those proposals ever tempted me in the slightest. What happened was not me, but we each have our own price to pay for the parts we play. The shame from that evening weighed heavily on me for many years.

I had already decided in my heart to leave that lifestyle behind. I had surrendered to God and asked for help. Deep down, I had always been a good girl, no matter what I was pretending to be or who I was trying to hurt by being destructive, and I couldn't let that night go.

Burdened by sorrow and shame, I opened my bible, praying God would speak to me, and it opened it directly to this scripture. It read, "Know this, God has even forgotten some of your sin" (Job 11:6, NIV). That's what I needed to hear at that moment, and no other version says it exactly the same. Sure, I knew he would forgive me. But in that moment, I needed to know he wasn't holding it over my head so I could stop beating myself up over it. I promise you that God will meet you wherever you are.

My popaw, a Southern Baptist preacher, once told me that I had brought a great deal of shame to my family, and to never disclose all the details from my past with my future husband. He said my husband would hold it against me. With this instilled in me, even before that night, I felt I was beyond redemption and that no good man would ever want me. But I longed for unconditional love and yearned to feel completely understood.

While my grandfather instructed me to hide my past from my future husband, in my heart, I questioned this. Deep down, I didn't think this was the way it had to go. I asked my cousin Taylor what she thought. She assured me, "The person God has in store for you will be someone with whom you can share everything." And she was right.

Dane has never made me feel dirty or ashamed of my past. He knows every dark detail. When I inquired why his beliefs differ from those of other good men, like my popaw, who would've judged me for my past, he responded, "I just don't feel that because someone makes a bad decision that makes them worthless. And I don't believe you should throw them away."

I share all this with you because I am not the only one with sexual trauma. Whether it is shame you or someone you care about is holding onto from rape, promiscuity, or both—I want you to know that it is ok to feel what we feel—but in the end, our shame is meant to be released. We are not to blame for our shame. I also need you to know that there exists a man God has set aside who will never make you feel less than because of any mistakes you might have made.

God can love and hold us through others. Out of all the men I could have ended up with, Dane is the one God had for me. The proof of the love I have been blessed with—from my husband to my children—makes evident the redeeming power of God's love. If *this* girl deserved a love on this earth by a man who doesn't judge and from a God that even forgets, it's time you forgive yourself. You are worthy, flaws and all. And with the right mindset, everything you touch can turn to gold.

Months before my relapse, I had been placed on a prayer list that was put on a projector during New Beginnings Sunday services. Our egos may cringe at the thought of being so far gone in your addiction that you are on a church's prayer list, but my heart felt loved and cared for. I was not embarrassed in the state I was in. It was exactly what I had needed. I ended up seeing it with my own eyes when I began attending shortly after the incident that took me decades to fully forgive myself for.

Things had begun to change for me when I was thirty-seven years old. I experienced an epiphany. I had begun to study the nervous system with a life coach and had realized that everything that I did was to survive—it all kept me alive. There were years I had spent blaming my younger self. I just couldn't forgive her. I couldn't share my story beyond a few brief moments of excruciating courage because I was deeply ashamed of her for the things she had done. I wish I had known sooner that I deserved my own forgiveness and compassion as much as anyone else.

I can tell you exactly where I was sitting in my office when the light bulb went off in my head. This was the first time I was able to thank my inner child and my nervous system for doing what it needed to survive at the time." I quietly said to her, "You kept me from taking my life." And through my gratitude and healing tears, I was finally able to forgive all parts of myself and see her in a new light.

From that day forward, I not only forgave her. I honored every part of her.

Trauma is the *lasting* imprint of an incident or many incidents that threatened our safety, sense of self, and/or ability to regulate our emotions and navigate relationships. Trauma negatively impacts the nervous system leaving us unable to regulate ourselves. For years I was either feeling stuck and frozen, or defensive and in fight or flight mode.

When I was in a hyperarousal state, I was unable to "just relax." My nervous system was conditioned to exist in a state of fear. I constantly felt anxious and was easily triggered. A healthier person can experience a stressful event, feel that stress move through them, and then after the event is over calm down by regulating themselves. I still struggle calming myself back down and not needing to self-medicate with sweets due to unresolved trauma. I am still healing as it comes up. Today, I may eat too many sweets in response to feeling overstimulated, but that's not where I hope to be a year from now.

I face my issues. And then I heal.

My "window of tolerance" has grown immensely. This is a concept in psychology that describes the range of emotional arousal within which a person can function effectively. When we are within this range, we can respond to stressors or challenges in a balanced way, maintaining a sense of control and clarity.

Operating within this window allows for effective processing of information and healthy engagement in relationships. This is where we can effectively manage our emotions, thoughts, and behaviors. However, exposure to overwhelming stress or trauma can push us outside of this window, resulting in a state of hyperarousal or hypoarousal—marked by feelings of anxiety, numbness, or disengagement. Recognizing and understanding our window of tolerance can be beneficial for developing coping strategies, improving emotional regulation, and enhancing our overall mental health.

I have learned that what I need when I am in a hyperarousal state is to calm down my parasympathetic nervous system. What helps me best is going on walks in nature. I also love yoga because in addition to movement, within this practice there is breathwork and meditation. This is my most powerful resource for relaxation, as all three are soothing for our nervous system.

You are in a hypoarousal state when you feel stuck, and even a little depressed, or a lot. You may not want to get out of bed. You may feel tired and lethargic. You may want to cry, but you can't. You feel frozen; that's why they call it the freeze state. When this is the case, the remedy is activating the parasympathetic nervous system.

To activate the parasympathetic nervous system, get out there and serve. Stick to your daily habits. Drink your water. Get to the gym. You can also try the technique of tapping your lips with two fingers because the lips are rich with parasympathetic fibers, and it may help you unfreeze. If you have children or can engage with them, play can be beneficial as well.

Would you believe that when we begin committing to these healthy practices long enough instead of our old harmful habits, we rewire our neural pathways? Rewiring neural pathways refers to the process of changing the way neurons communicate and form connections in the brain. This concept is rooted in neuroplasticity, which is the brain's ability to adapt and reorganize itself in response to new experiences, learning, or injury. When we engage in new activities, learn new information, or change our behaviors, we can strengthen existing neural pathways or create new ones.

I once would escape the house and my husband during a fight to drink margaritas by myself. Now, in my most triggered state, I may or may not have jumped out of Dane's car at a stop sign coming off the interstate ramp like an unhinged human when our fight escalated on Easter of 2024, but rather than drinking, I opted for a long walk in nature instead.

Our argument centered around his insistence that I was not to eat a piece of the chicken we had purchased to take to his aunt's house. When I went to get a piece anyway, he snatched the box of chicken and biscuits from my hands and held it on his side of the car, out of my reach, while insulting me with an unkind name. Now, my instinct at this stage in my healing after implementing new habits and rewiring my neural pathways may still be to escape a triggering situation—but I am proud to say I no longer run away to alcohol.

I still feel this strong desire to flee when I am deeply activated, but leaving alcohol out of the equation has helped immensely. My husband has also learned his own lesson. As long as he doesn't withhold food from me when I am hungry, insult me, yell at me, or treat me like a child—we will remain friends.

There is another old saying, what helps you survive is not what's going to help you thrive. The modalities that helped me cope and stay alive—the drugs, the alcohol, the relationships, the running away—all helped to keep me here. But if I want to blossom and bloom to the next level, I have to continue healing from the past and forgive myself. That's a journey I am still on today.

I encourage you to take your time forgiving others, including yourself. It is a process that doesn't happen overnight. You must get humble. It's okay to admit you didn't have all the answers. It's okay to learn, relearn, and ask for help.

Straighten Your Crown Exercises:

- Write a letter to your inner child, thanking them.
- Write a letter to the adult version of yourself, forgiving them.
- When you feel you are in a hyperarousal state, try deep breathing, meditation, yoga, essential oils, a warm bath, a hot shower, and/or talk to someone.
- When you are in a hypoarousal state, limit your screen time, get outdoors, tap your lips with two fingers, exercise, serve in your community, lie on the grass and identify something within your line of sight to focus on which will help center you, and/or talk to someone.

CHAPTER

Seven

Beauty Is Only Skin Deep—A Queen Takes Care of Herself

Being a Queen requires more than getting your nails done, facials, and for some of us, a little filler. Don't get me wrong, that is all fun to do, and something we may choose to pamper ourselves with to feel our most confident. However, true self-care goes much deeper than professionally styled hair and gorgeous lashes that make your eyes pop.

Before I could become serious about taking myself to the next level—to thrive, not only survive—I had to become devoted to my self-care routine, which was healing and regulating my nervous system. To me, it's more than nails or hair or what society deems as "self-care." It's about nurturing my body, mind, and soul.

A pivotal moment for me was when I read the book *Untamed* by Glennon Doyle. Her book inspired me to form a connection to God based on my own terms—not religion. For years, I didn't talk to God or pray. I was no longer convinced of things I was taught or traumatized from seeing as a child. I threw the baby out with the bath water. Doyle's book invited my faith back in and it is presently one of the most precious cornerstones of my life.

Her book also inspired me to give up alcohol. As I mentioned earlier, even after I had married the man of my dreams and gave birth to his children, I still relied on drinking. I recognized it was holding me back from becoming the highest version of myself—the woman I felt a calling to be over a decade prior when *Celia's Eyes* poured out of me. Although alcohol hadn't seriously hurt my life, marriage, or career—yet—I knew if I didn't stop it or get it under control, I could potentially lose everything.

Alcohol is sneaky like that. You don't think it's causing your anxiety, depression, and impulsiveness, but it is. However, through eliminating this last means of the many ways I have so cleverly escaped myself, I found it to be the first step in another radical transformation in my life.

When I quit alcohol, I took my power back completely.

A month after ending my journey with alcohol, I began working with Elizabeth, an energy kinesiologist trained in Chinese energy medicine. I reached out to her, hoping she could help me access my voice. I instinctively understood that expressing my voice was the next step in my journey, but fear was holding me back. She helped me co-regulate as she was remarkably balanced and serene. I was very drawn to simply being in her presence. I kept my mind open, and I trusted her to help me.

It was during my initial visit with her that I expressed my concern that my voice might be blocked. Some may refer to that as the throat chakra, but to me and my vernacular at the time, I referred to it as "voice." She said her intuition was telling her that an incident had occurred when I was fifteen that made me feel "repulsed." She said it was an event that caused my soul to detach and split off—or in psychology, disassociate. I told her my mom gave me my last spanking at sixteen while my second stepfather watched. I remember looking at him in disgust. But Elizabeth said, "No, this event took place when you were fifteen." I told her I couldn't recall, and we continued.

She had me lie down on a bed as she performed, "what the shamans call a soul retrieval." I kept my eyes closed as she circled around me and prayed. It felt relaxing to be in her presence, but it didn't feel like anything was happening. This practice is based on the belief that during times of trauma, a part of the soul can flee the body to survive. The goal of the shaman or energy worker is to find and integrate the missing soul parts back into the client's energy field which can heal them on a physical, energetic, and soul level.

During the same same week I met her, I felt liberated enough to launch my podcast, *Love Waits for You,* which became a vehicle to explore my shadow work. I am a firm believer that those who feel heard begin to heal. The first season of my podcast focused on my journey toward self-worth and healing by confronting the trauma I had hidden.

Looking back, I can see her mission was fulfilled.

Shadow work is a type of psychotherapy that involves facing ourselves—including the parts we often hide, especially the trauma. Shadow work can be challenging and, at times, deeply unsettling. In my view, engaging in shadow work feels similar to the experience of competing in a pageant as an adult, as it forces you to confront both your strengths *and* vulnerabilities head-on.

This is why I became so captivated by pageantry. Yes, there is a younger, unhealed version of myself that did not get enough attention as a child, and shining on a stage *does* fulfill a deep-seated need to be seen, but its significance extends far beyond the surface. I look forward to the spiritual quantum leaping and the self-development in a "high-pressure cooker" as one of my sisters referred to it. Each time I have ever broken down—I broke through into an even more healed, evolved, expansive, and compassionate version of myself.

Speaking of spirituality, let's go back to the "shamanic soul retrieval." You may be wondering, *Did you ever recall the "incident" that made you feel "repulsed"? Was your soul ever "retrieved"?*

I had launched my podcast within the very first week of meeting Elizabeth. But it was on Episode 4, *May I Have Your Attention, Please?*, that I felt led to go into explicit detail of the sexual abuse I had experienced as a barely fifteen-year-old girl. In that episode, I was continuing to catch listeners up on my past. I didn't call it abuse, and I even referred to the thirty-seven-year-old man who had been an employee of my mother since I was seven years old as a "gentleman." The main focus of the episode was to illustrate how our desire for attention often originates in childhood.

After that episode was released, my husband listened to it and appeared unwell. I chose not to ask him why, fearing he might express something negative about my openness and vulnerability with my "lovely listeners."

The following morning, I found it difficult to get out of bed. I wasn't educated in the trauma responses to recognize that I was experiencing a freeze state. By discussing the abuse, I had inadvertently retraumatized myself. I was brand new to sobriety and healing these deeper layers. I didn't understand what was happening to me.

My husband came home to my lying on the grass in the middle of our front lawn to find some sort of relief. He teased me, "You look crazy, what are the neighbors going to think?" Then I fell apart. I told him I didn't understand why grief had come over me out of nowhere.

Being the grounding and healing presence in my life, he said, "Celia, you mentioned on your podcast yesterday that you were abused, and you are still blaming yourself. Any girl or woman who listens to you might end up blaming herself too. That's a heavy burden to carry, and it's no surprise you're not feeling well."

It had been two years since my mom and first stepdad divorced when the "incident" occurred that left me feeling "repulsed." I was working at my mom's furniture store during the summer of 2000. An older man, someone I had known since I was seven, would often pick me up from school in the furniture delivery truck as he was one of my mother's employees. However, that summer I turned fifteen, he began to focus on me in a way that I had never experienced before.

I found his attention addictive, as it gave me a sense of power from his interest. Now I realize why it affected me so deeply. I felt unable to control the boards shifting beneath me between the divorces and the constant arrival and departure of new father figures. I questioned my worthiness of their attention, believing that if I were truly valuable, they would have stayed. Yet in this situation, I discovered a fleeting sense of control and power.

When he would ask me to pull my skirt up higher, I felt gross inside, you could even say, "repulsed." Although I would tell him no, that didn't stop me from walking by him in hopes of receiving more of his compliments, despite the fact they made me feel dirty. He was meeting a need inside of me that longed specifically for male attention, no matter if it was good or bad.

This is why I blamed myself for twenty-two years. I had enjoyed his attention all the while knowing it was wrong. Every day I would come home and record what was going on in my diary. I wrote about how guilty I had felt, but that I couldn't stop it, and I was afraid of where it was going. Now that I am his age, I say shame on him. He saw my vulnerability. As an easy prey, I became his target.

He was aware that I was a virgin, and since I had not yet developed, his attraction to me does not make sense—unless he was a pedophile. I can't shake the fear that he may have had the chance to try and groom others as well.

All the talk and teasing eventually led up to an afternoon where he had one of my mom's other employees guard the warehouse entrance. Then, he begged me to come back to the warehouse with him, much like my children pleading for their iPad before dinner. Once inside, he kissed me and began to digitally rape me. Less than three seconds later, I jerked away and rushed past the other man he had stationed as a lookout. I found refuge alone in the bathroom at the front of the expansive 30,000 square foot building— the same building I had driven my Barbie car through as a little girl and had practically grown up in. This building, where I would rarely visit again, now housed a part of my soul that I would be separated from for the next twenty-two years.

I ran straight to the bathroom to cry with my mother just doors away locked in her office, but the tears didn't surface. I thought I was going to get sick, but I never did. I am so thankful I wasn't attracted to him otherwise he could have been more successful in pursuing me. Imagine the trauma I would have to heal from if I had fallen for the child predator?

Thank God I got away. Even though I had left part of my soul in that bathroom that day.

After the abuse, I stopped working for my mother so I wouldn't have to see him again, and she never asked why. I had begun cutting my left forearm out of curiosity. I also started going to parties that I never was interested in before and sneaking out at night. I felt like something was inherently wrong with me after the sexual abuse, but I couldn't place my finger on it. I had completely disassociated. I didn't know why I felt this way until I was thirty-seven years old.

After my mom read my diary and discovered what her employee had done, she took immediate action and confronted him, ultimately firing him in front of his wife, who also worked for her. I ended up facing consequences as well. She pulled me out of school and isolated me at home for three weeks, allowing no contact with anyone but herself. Eventually, I reached a breaking point and stole her car and ran away to my dad's in Pennsylvania at fifteen.

I believe what hurt me the most when finally processing this trauma was facing the fact that my mother didn't go to the police—she did nothing to protect me or advocate for me when she found out. Despite having evidence of his confession, she even hired him back. I had become numb to many things as a teenager, but I could still feel that blow.

When I confronted her about it for the first time at thirty-seven years old, she said, she only "partially" held me responsible, in her defense. Now that I am a mother, it's hard to give her grace for this. I will always have my children's backs. I will always advocate for them. They will always be my precious beings. I believe I am here on this earth to love and protect them. I have a hard time forgiving my mother for knowing she read in my diary that I was abused by her employee, but instead of rushing to embrace me and get me the help I desperately needed, she punished and blamed me. I carried that shame with me for twenty-two years until my heart and soul were ready to see and process the truth.

I stopped having a relationship with her once I began facing and healing this trauma because it triggered me *too* much. I do believe in facing our traumas and that our triggers are an invitation to heal, but we are not required to befriend our abusers. We do not have to remain in a relationship with them, even if they are family. Doing so, would push us out beyond our window of tolerance. If it hurts, we can distance ourselves while we heal. We can love and forgive them from afar.

Creating distance between my mom and I, as painful as it felt, was the best decision for my mental health. There was a significant amount of emotional abuse that had occurred, but in regard to the neglect, I know she was unable to offer me more than she could provide for herself. I will never understand her, but I commit to forgiving her, for myself.

I began writing this book in July of 2022. I was in the midst of writing and recording my podcast when it suddenly struck me what had actually happened. Following what felt like a truck had run over me the day after recording *My I Have Your Attention, Please?*, Dane had to fly out of town for his work and leave me in my inconsolable grief.

I still managed to care for my children, a much easier task to do—if I don't say so myself—sober and healing trauma than it was wasted and not. My therapist says my ability to face my trauma and grieve within the same day that I can also play and be present with my children—that is what integration looks like and is evidence of my good mental health. Maybe that makes you feel better, too.

As I journaled after dropping my children off at preschool, I confronted the harsh reality of the molestation I had experienced. Within hours, I realized the sexual trauma was the source of all my self-hatred. It was *the* root. I never struggled with feelings of inadequacy and self-hatred until that happened. Years of questions and reflections suddenly coalesced, providing me with answers all at once.

I was processing that one of my parents knew about it, blamed me, and didn't label it as abuse. The other parent, I realized, may have also been aware. I was scared to feel betrayal, times two. But in a fit of ballistic rage, I called my dad sobbing. I told him about the abuse for the first time and asked him if he knew, and if so, why he never informed the police. He claimed he had no idea and was extremely upset that my mom had kept this from him.

I am careful to not throw around the word "crazy," because in my most unstable emotional moments, I questioned my sanity—when in truth—I was going back in time and saving myself. At thirty-seven years old in what honestly felt like a manic state, while my babies were at preschool, I drove to the Hendersonville Police Station and shared my story. I instinctively went to advocate for "little Celia" realizing no one had done so before.

Trauma isn't bound by time. When you face it, and really process it, the pain doesn't have any concept of it. I was in hysteria over a trauma that happened twenty-two years ago, and only someone who has been in this position or a trained psychologist would truly understand. Although the police officer was compassionate, I am sure she was equally confused. She sympathetically shared with me that I would need to contact the police department in the city where the abuse took place.

From their parking lot, I contacted the South Pittsburg Police Station. I called to arrange an in-person appointment to file a report that Monday after the weekend. I was aware it had been twenty-two years, but I had to do this *for* her. I had to advocate for *her*. I was not wrong in that it's never too late.

Not to my surprise, the officer knew exactly who I was and was familiar with my family. He said he walked in on my mom at her mission throwing up "demons" in a trash can when DCS was called. People in the community were concerned about "the kids" (me and my siblings). It was their determination that she was a mess over separating from my first stepdad, but not in too bad of shape for us to be taken away. As a trained CASA (Court Appointed Special Advocate for children) Volunteer, I understand they did all they could do.

The most uncomfortable and I'll say it, crazed, part of my healing was that Friday without the grounding presence of my husband. He was *also* unavailable by phone all day. I had gone from dealing with grief that morning when we spoke—to unconsolable rage—to attempting to file a police report—and ultimately being on a full-blown mission to rescue "little Celia" by the time he had talked to me that evening. But my husband never made me feel crazy. He intuitively knew I was healing, *and* he also knew he was flying back home the next day and that I would be ok.

However, my dad was sincerely worried about me. He was afraid I was having a nervous breakdown and begged me to quit the podcast. He said I was retraumatizing myself.

And he wasn't wrong.

When I got off the phone with my dad that Sunday, I almost had a panic attack. From seeing my mom lose control because of her mental illness, out of fear, I asked my husband, "Is that what is happening to me? Am I going to have a nervous breakdown? Is my dad, right?" I sobbed uncontrollably outside our favorite sushi restaurant with my two babies in the back seat completely unphased.

While I was overwhelmed with fear of the unknown, he reminded me as he so often lovingly does, that I was the strongest person he had ever met, and he knew I was just purging. He told me I was in control of this and said that I needed to keep letting it out. He was right.

It's wild how the mind is fragile like that, because if he had been even slightly anxious or fearful, I would've let myself continue drowning in the "what ifs" and had a full-blown panic attack. Instead, I received his co-regulation and comforting words. And I allowed myself to be held by him. Once my tears dried, we had one of the most memorable dinner dates with our family.

The following morning, we drove two hours to my hometown police station where I reported my abuse and the abuser to a female officer who understood exactly what I was going through. The police station was two blocks from where it had happened. After that, it was finally over. I felt the closure I needed. I did what I had to do. I understood that nothing might come of it, but I would be ready to confront him as an adult, especially with my husband by my side. I didn't have that support back then, and that scumbag knew it. He was far from a gentleman.

I had begun meditating and practicing mindfulness after I had healed this root trauma. I would do my best to set aside time each day to shut off and organize the chatter of my mind to the best of my ability whether through meditation, yoga, or journaling. This time spent alone was invaluable because it helped me understand I was not defined by my thoughts. I was able to sit and observe, rather than identify with them. As a result, I became calmer and more intentional, specifically about only sharing from my authentic voice. I embraced being vulnerable on social media more. I didn't allow the lack of likes to keep me from sharing what was on and in my heart.

Part of being mindful is being intentional. I say "No, thank you" more now than I ever have. I check in with my body throughout the day. I ask myself, "How do I feel?" or "How is this making me feel?" Much of our lives are spent on autopilot if we don't pause and check in with ourselves. As one of my brothers advised me during an emotionally trying time, "Be where your feet are."

Gratitude is another mindfulness practice. Whether at church or on my own, I sing praise and worship music. By never letting myself forget where I have come from and how God has always had his hand on my life, I remain humble, grounded, and grateful. Gratitude is among the highest vibrational frequencies one can achieve. It will strengthen you.

I do my best to rise above the comparison game. Best advice until you get there—and just know I am "getting there" with you—know your limits. With social media, it makes it more difficult. Unfollow or mute the stories and posts if you need to for the sake of bringing your best self and most optimal mental health. Sometimes social media can feel like information overload. Self-care is having a deep care and focus on yourself. True self-care is revolutionary.

Mind you, I don't have it all together, but I keep at it. Self-care is accepting your flaws. Sure, strive to be better, but we must meet and love ourselves where we are. I don't allow the pressure of perfection to hold me back. I finally feel free to be myself and it has been time I share not only through the written word, but to grow my community, through my spoken words.

The greatest thing about self-care is that as soon as I started to truly take care of myself—by eliminating alcohol first and foremost—I was able to get quiet, settle in, and face myself (instead of repeating old patterns and escaping). And it was because of this, all the dreams and visions I had for my most ideal self—that they had begun to come true.

Presently, I lift heavy weights for fun, practice yoga, drink my water, swim, bike, run, and I eat and move in a way that makes me feel my best 80% of the time. That 20% of the time is less restrictive, and I am still learning moderation. All the above—including the 20%—to me, is self-care, too.

The way I see it, if you truly feel good, keep doing what you're doing. All the changes and transformations I've made have come from a place of pain. I no longer wanted to hurt. I have overcome so much because I had to, but I remain a work in progress. I don't have all the answers, but I will share everything that has helped me along the way for the rest of my life.

Ever since I quit alcohol over two years ago, I have been struggling with sugar binges. Sugar binging affects the dopamine levels in our brain and the crash (for me) negatively impacts my mental health. It is so easy to justify in our sick society because it isn't a drug or alcohol.

What does a sugar hangover for me feel like? I want to cry out of helplessness for feeling bad. I force myself to work out which lifts the gloom a little, but not enough. By day three, sober from sugar, I start to feel better. The veil has lifted, and my vibrant highest self is returning.

I've gone two months straight without any processed sugar and then Halloween rolled around. It isn't even about managing my weight. It is about the cloud of despair that comes over me when I do too much that isn't good for me. My body is very sensitive like that. Maybe yours, too, if you check in.

Giving ourselves grace is essential while we keep our eyes on the prize (our best self) and our minds open, so we remain self-aware. Life is about evolving, we weren't born having it all figured out and spoiler alert, we never arrive. Even the ones who may look like they have it all together, do not. When you are deeply committed to your growth and evolution, being painstakingly self-aware is a part of it.

I encourage you to continually seek ways to improve while embracing and loving yourself as you are.

And finally, I practice self-care by leading with love and compassion versus judgment towards myself and others as I continue sharing my story. You may think how is that self-care? Because as I have told you before, *serving others feeds you first.*

What exactly does it feed you? When I serve, it feeds me joy. Although energy is being taken, life is being given. When I first began traveling the country to host workshops, I would drive four hours one way and feel like I was never closer to my purpose. I founded a nonprofit from this feeling. Sharing my story and it being received so well has been incredibly healing.

Straighten Your Crown Exercises:

- Establish a self-care routine and rituals that honor where you are and make it easy to encourage self-care as a daily practice.
- Investigate various healing modalities—somatic, energy work, yoga, meditation, sound therapy, etc.
- Read books on self-help, trauma, and how the nervous system works.
- Consider hiring a life and/or energy coach—who can hold you accountable and check-in on your progress.
- Invite friends, your partner, and/or spouse into participating in the rituals and routines, so your total environment encourages healing.

CHAPTER

Eight

Find Your Fire—Do the Impossible

When I was on drugs, my father gave me somewhat of an ultimatum. I couldn't have a relationship with him or his family, in person, until I proved I was well enough to graduate college. He didn't want to expose my darkness to his children, my brothers. That may sound harsh to you, but God uses everything for good. That was the kind of tough love I needed. Although technically, he didn't make me wait that long.

The same day my dad was informed that I was almost murdered, was the same day he discovered I had gotten married to a man I had only known for three weeks. His heart broke and it softened towards me. He felt guilty as it had been over five years since he had seen me. He realized it was time to intervene. But I was not ready, and that only made his heart hurt worse.

You see, when we reconnected, it was only the first day after my separation from my ex, following the worst of his abuse. My ex had already sobered up, called me from jail, and we were back together. He was remorseful, like always. I knew in his heart of hearts that he didn't want to do the things he did to me. He didn't have to convince me of that.

During the brief time we were together, I endured his verbal and physical abuse. He had experienced my wrath back in words as well. When it had first started happening, my boss at the bar where I was working told me to leave him because it was only going to get worse, but I didn't listen. There were *only* some small bruises behind my bottom lip from being slapped. Then a few big bruises on my arm from being punched after *I* called *him* a name during a fight. That still wasn't bad enough to drive me away. I could also justify being manhandled, slapped, and pushed around every time he drank, which was every day. I believed I could control him and help manage his drinking, but I was mistaken.

I was in that relationship for the rest of my life, as far as I was concerned. I was determined not to give up on him. Leaving him in his illness to suffer alone was never part of the plan.

He would wake up in the morning after his alcohol binges with the shakes. He was in serious trouble. Addiction is something you can't overcome without a fight, which he wasn't willing to do. Nothing was worth the fight—not me, himself, or our marriage that was soon annulled.

God speaks to my heart. Anytime I act on the impressions, everything flows. It was May of 2006 that the door incident occurred. I was twenty-one years old.

The fight started over me nagging him about drinking with one of his friends he had over. He was only supposed to have a couple of drinks. By then, he was over six in. Because I was codependent, it was my job to monitor and take care of him.

While arguing, he broke my phone due to his aggressive behavior. So, then I took his flip phone, looked him in the eye, and broke it in half on purpose. Things from there spiraled fast. He still had a friend over at this point when he picked me up and hurled me to the ground in the kitchen. This caused me to get whiplash from the back of my neck hitting the bottom of the cabinets. Then, he forced me into our bedroom where he climbed on top of me and began hitting me. His friend ran back to the bedroom as I was screaming for help. We locked eyes as I begged him to call the police. But with a frightened to death look in his own eyes that mirrored mine, he fled the scene.

I had kept pepper spray on me as protection because of his violent outbursts. At this point, I had to use it to get him off me. But it didn't even slow him down. It only infuriated him further.

He immediately ran to the other side of the bedroom and snatched the door off its hinges in a raging fit. The first time he had thrown the door at me, I had shielded my face and head the best I could, although it still made an impact. The second time, he came right up to me, lifted the door up, then bashed me in the back of my head with it. In that position, I could only duck, which didn't shield anything.

When I stood up after the assault, I immediately panicked. The blood scared me. It was saturating my clothes from running down the back of my head and my face. I can recall how I felt when I saw my face for the first time. I should have been scared, but the fighter in me was livid. The side of my face instantly bugled out the size of a baseball. As soon as I got up to see my swollen and bloody face in the dresser mirror, I started screaming and said to him, "Look at what you did!"

He then picked me up and dragged me into the bathroom where he shoved me into the shower to clean up because the mess was "disgusting." I then returned to a state of panic instead of anger. My tone changed as I tried to assure him, "It is okay, baby, really. I'm not mad." In my mind, I hoped to trick him into calming down.

His response was, "Oh, no, no. You've messed with the wrong one!"

While in the shower, where I stood in shock—I was now scared to death. I didn't even clean the mess because I could only stand there frozen. I had no game plan in mind, no way out. I didn't know what to do. It wasn't that I couldn't take what had just happened because I was still standing—the door didn't kill me.

Although I was processing the events and was shook up by them, that part was over. It was the overwhelming fear of what was going to come next that had me terrified.

A few minutes after he had forced me into the shower, he hadn't calmed down from his rage like he usually would. He took my pepper spray and used it on me while shouting and hitting me. When he walked out, my heart sank. It was then that I understood he wasn't going to let me leave. There was no hope or escape—this was it. I genuinely felt I wasn't going to live through the experience because I couldn't see a way out.

As I stared down at the drain, crying out to God in my heart and aloud, I was certain that was how it was all going to end for me. I still hadn't reunited with my dad. I was far from restoration and feeling redeemed. I wasn't a college graduate. I was off drugs and in church trying to live right, but there I found myself in another pit of despair.

What I did have—that I wasn't as sure of as I am today— is the unexplainable, undeniable, almighty God by my side.

It was a very specific moment in time that I can still see in my mind's eye—while staring at the shower drain, God told my heart, in response to my cries for help, to "Go now." It wasn't a panicked urging; it was calm and assured. It came out of nowhere, but it was perfectly timed by a God who was in control of that moment and those to come. I recognized it was him, and only because I chose to listen, I believe that I am alive to write to you today.

As soon as my heart heard, "Go now," I left the shower running and tiptoed out with only a towel to cover me. As I quietly closed the door behind me, I noticed he was two rooms away on the balcony, attempting to repair his cell phone. I found a spot to hide in the corner of the dining room, as I waited for him to check on me in the shower so I could make my escape. I could see the front door, and it was unlocked. I was relieved because that would save me time not having to unlock it, which I needed. When I saw him start to make his way towards the bathroom to check on me, I knew it was my moment. As soon as he turned the knob and took his first step into the bathroom, I fled for my life.

As I watched the police escort him away, a wave of guilt washed over me. They said he was asleep when they went in to arrest him. He claimed he couldn't remember what had happened, insisting he had blacked out.

I still can't shake the image of blood on the walls of our apartment when we returned home. It resembled a murder scene in the bedroom. I don't know if being a drug addict was worse or that.

He had violated the terms of his intensive probation, and I would soon learn even bigger than that. Just a day away from completing his 11/29 probation, the timing of the assault meant we would be forced apart for two years while he served time. This felt like a curse. In hindsight, I now see it as another miracle.

I wish I could say I came to my senses and found the strength in me to leave him on my own. I am sure I would feel immense pride—knowing myself and my human nature's desire to feel superior where I can. But the void, my wounds, my trauma, the ache I was left with in his absence was too painful to bear. I called it love. But it truly wasn't. We were walking addictions feeding off each other. We were entwined in a cycle of dependency, like parasites drawing sustenance from one another.

Think about it. Who in their right mind meets a guy and marries him three weeks later? After the night of my relapse and sexual assault, I resolved to remain celibate until marriage. Well, he wasn't willing to wait more than three weeks to become intimate. And back then, I was simply thrilled that *anyone* wanted to marry me.

When we met, I even overlooked that he was on intensive probation for alcohol and drug-related charges. I was not naïve to the fact that he had assaulted cops, kicked the window in a cop car out when they had arrested him, and had just been released from jail when met. However, when he had told me he had gotten saved in jail, *that* was my green light. And the fact that he was even willing to wait those three weeks to sleep with me? That's more than the guys who had played me in my past. It must have been true love.

You see, I didn't love myself back then, so it was easy to convince myself that having someone who wanted to marry and love me, rather than use me, was a positive thing. My mind and the way it worked still needed a lot of healing. But I don't shame her. Aren't we all just doing the best we can with what we have?

When I looked at him, I saw he was a wounded soul like my own. I felt I could show him that I was once in his shoes, tell him my pain, what I had been through, and encourage him to overcome it, too. He was my project.

Although I never struggled with rage, I related to him. He had his childhood stolen. I knew what that felt like, and I also knew how it felt to be misunderstood. He didn't feel he had a choice, and I remembered how that felt to not want to engage in harmful behaviors, yet still feel compelled to do them. I knew what hating myself felt like. We both knew how worthlessness felt.

After all, the same trauma that did it to me did it to him.

I've learned that this caretaking behavior of mine was all rooted from my childhood. I was a caretaker to my mother's emotional needs growing up. I was recreating a relationship I was familiar with, a relationship where I met their needs for them to meet mine—a codependent relationship where I had the power and was the caretaker because I was the stronger one. And in return, I received love.

At the court hearing in November of 2006, when the chancellor granted me an annulment on the grounds that I was deceived into a marriage with a man who was in jail for assaulting me—the moment he said my ex's full name and dissolved what was—I ran out in tears. That was the morning before a night left alone in the bathtub with my thoughts dreaming for death, once again.

When he was initially incarcerated, I let him dictate my schedule, ensuring I was home at specific times to take his calls throughout the day. I made it to each visitation and wrote letters, all while remaining devoted to our relationship. I had lost my job when I had to call out for the abuse from the man my boss had told me months before I needed to leave. I was now burdened with the hospital bills, along with our expenses, which were all in my name. As a result, my credit score plummeted, and I found myself in a major bind.

I don't know what led me to call my cousin, Graham, who was an attorney and seek advice. There must have been a seed of life and hope sprouting within me. As much as I hated myself, this wasn't a life even I could ever endure.

Graham and his wife, Sharon, offered me a place to stay at their home, assist with my bills, and help me find a job. Graham also offered to represent me as my lawyer in an effort to secure an annulment, but under one condition: I had to cut off all contact with him. I was backed into a corner. I had no other choice.

When I had to end all communication without providing an explanation, I felt like I had abandoned him. I assured him that I would wait for him before he went to jail, and I truly meant it. But fate intervened on my behalf through Graham—and even the timing of the incident itself.

Once I had settled in at Graham and Sharon's, my dad arranged and covered the cost of my flight to visit him, my stepmom, and my three brothers. We finally reunited after being apart for five years.

After this, his love and support strengthened me, and I graduated with a bachelor's degree three years later at the age of twenty-four. I knew he had desired this for me, and that it would make us both proud. He had high expectations, and there was a part of me still alive inside that also had them for myself.

At the age of twenty-four, I was employed by Blue Cross, having been free from meth and cocaine for four years, living a celibate lifestyle, and had recently graduated from college. But I knew if I wanted to heal the relationship with my father, mother, and brothers, I had to demonstrate to them that I was capable and that my transformation was here to stay. On a whim, and with the encouragement of a friend and mentor, Andrea, I decided to sign up for a work-sponsored 5K. What better way to show my father I had come full circle, than by showing him I trained for, ran, and finished a race? Granted, I had never run more than a mile in my life! But there is some kind of threshold I hit between mile one and mile three, and once I surpassed it, I felt like I could run forever.

What started as a mission to prove myself became a personal passion of mine. I soon discovered so much peace in running. I found I could run and cry—and just let it all out. My running shoes and the pavement didn't care if I was crying, if I wasn't perfect, or if I was defective, which I still felt. My running shoes didn't need me to prove anything. I could just run—like Forrest Gump, and just keep running. Eventually, I went from feeling so incredibly weak on the inside—from my dependence on drugs and not feeling like I could leave my abuser—to feeling full of power. Even though I wasn't very fast at that time, I had endurance. It was like a small candle had been lit inside me, and suddenly I was a girl on fire. I couldn't wait to go out for a run every day.

After that 5K, I had signed up and began training for a full marathon. Then I was competing in triathlons and placing. It wasn't long before the strength I felt in my body manifested in every aspect of my life. With this newfound passion—running and pushing myself—I finally felt strong. My insides matched my outsides. The more I put myself out there and challenged myself, the more I felt accomplished. And the more accomplished I felt, the more self-respect and self-love I found. It had been within me all along.

Running helped me shed the previous version of myself, so the Celia I had always been meant to be, could emerge. After ten years of running multiple marathons, countless 5K's, and over a dozen triathlons, in the past several years I have qualified to compete on a national level among the highest ranked amateur triathletes in the country. When I compete at nationals, I land directly in the middle of the best non-professional triathletes every year. And for the first time in my life, I have someone there to support me and cheer me on, my husband and even sometimes children.

And yes, my father—and everyone else—could see the transformation from the inside out. Most importantly, by finding my passion, I realized I can do anything—and I mean *anything*—I put my mind to. Pageants would even one day follow.

Why not compete at the state and national level? Why not me? I also started to write another book, where I discovered once again, I loved to write. We can all do what our mind thinks is "impossible" if we put ourselves out there and just try.

After my first 5K I was hooked. When I shared with my friend Andrea that I hoped to improve enough to place in the races one day, she exclaimed, "You can!" And she was right. Anyone can do anything if their passion and purpose are aligned.

I am passionate about running, and my purpose is to be the best version of myself—to be wholly, authentically Celia. With running, I was able to live my purpose—and with that I did what I thought was once impossible. And you can, too.

Straighten Your Crown Exercises:

- Find out what your passion is. Some people know it—it could be writing, creating, singing, acting, swimming, yoga, running a business, etc. Others don't—and if that is you, think back on your life and look at the times that made you come most alive, get lost in an activity, and feel at peace.
- Get curious about your passions—you don't have to be passionate about a single thing. Maybe you haven't found it, or you may have multiple passions. I didn't discover running until someone encouraged me to try it. Soon I discovered triathlons, Orangetheory, pageants, writing books, and podcasts. You don't have to be passionate about just one thing! Maybe there are dancing classes, pottery classes, or physical challenges that you've been curious about, but never thought you could do. You won't know unless you try.
- Consider what your purpose is in life. Everyone has a different purpose—but I think discovering it is essential to becoming whole again—so you can heal and live authentically. What do you think your purpose is? Are you living your life with purpose?
- Make a list of things that seem impossible to you, and consider, what if someone told you, "You can do it," like Andrea told me. Imagine your life if you did the impossible? What would that look like? How would that make you feel?

CHAPTER

Nine

Transform Your Pain into Power

I always wanted to be seen and heard. From a young age, something deep inside was calling out for help, for love, for attention. I didn't know it when I was a child, but that deep wound of not being held, felt, seen, and understood would one day be my calling, my salvation.

I recall feeling this way for the first time when I was a little more than two years old. Now I know most people say that people can't form memories that young, but I do remember this. The feeling was connected to one of my first memories of abuse as well. And as Dr. Bessel van der Kolk says, "the body keeps the score." And boy, did it.

On that particular day, my mother had her friend Carol over. When they were together, they always became lost in their conversations and quickly forgot about me. This infuriated two-year-old me. As any two-year-old, I wanted all eyes on me. So naturally, I kept interrupting them. I felt so jealous of Carol. My mother was only paying attention to her, and little Celia was not cool with it. So naturally, I pitched a fit, as my own young son Tristan is apt to do when he also wants his way.

My mother, unable to realize I needed comfort and attention, was not having it. Instead of acknowledging my existence, distracting me with an activity, or giving me a hug I clearly so desperately needed, she locked me in my room.

I was enraged! Immediately, I grabbed a yellow shag carpet covered pillow that was in the shape of a mound. If you're an 80's baby, you might have had one of them too. I strategically positioned it directly in front of the door. I propped myself up on it and with my legs pressed up against the door I started to kick my feet. I wasn't going to go gently in my room and keep myself occupied…that was not my way. Not even at two-years-old.

My stepfather, who was called to come handle me while he was in the middle of work and still wearing his overalls, busted through the door and jerked me up. He threw me in his truck and drove me to a barn. I kept on screaming and wailing. Nothing and no one were going to stop me. I was fighting mad, and I demanded to be heard. Once outside the barn, he threw me over a bale of hay, yanked my pants down, and began beating me. You would think I would have quickly changed my attitude and given up on my protests. But the more he hit me, the more I screamed and fought back. And consequently, he hit me harder. He couldn't break me. Nothing could break my resolve: I demanded to be heard, to be seen, to be loved. He couldn't hit it out of me. Even as my bottom became red and swollen, I would not yield. Eventually, he got tired of beating me before I got tired of screaming and fighting. He threw me back in the truck and delivered me back to my mother with no less fight in me than when he hauled off with me and beat me.

My heart breaks for that little innocent baby being beaten to bruises by an ignorant grown-up who didn't have the wherewithal to manage his own emotions, let alone mine. I often think of my own two boys—and can't imagine anyone treating them in the same way. It sickens me. And yet, there I was, little Celia with no one there to defend me. Not then. Not ever. And there were many more times he felt the need to put me in my place. That day, however, sticks in my mind forever. Because it was there, with no one to protect me and the world seemingly against me, something emerged in me.

In many ways, it was like that scene in *Superman*, when as a baby, he lifts a car. It was then he realized his own strength, his God-given superpower. But even Superman has his Kryptonite, the thing that brings him to his knees. And for me, that was the desperate need to be loved, held, seen, and heard. Of course, these are not extraordinary wishes for a child. Or anyone for that matter.

No, my mother never spanked me so hard I was left with bruises. But she didn't defend me either. She never protected me from those beatings. Even when the bruises were so clearly visible, she didn't intercede. It wasn't until her friend Carol of all people, the woman I despised as a child, threatened to report him to the police, that my mother finally made him stop. I can't tell you how many times I just wished for someone to whisk me away and hold me, protect me, cherish me, and love me.

At the time, my strong will to stop the injustice and have my voice heard felt more like a curse than a superpower. I mean, wouldn't you think I would have shut up after the first spank? Wouldn't anyone in their right mind stay quiet when they knew another hit was coming? But not me. I have often wondered why? What was inside me that kept fighting—that wanted so desperately to be heard and seen?

I realize now that pain and the subsequent curse of being a fighter and shouter were my special gifts, my superpowers. They are what kept me alive. They are what kept me fighting to survive—during my difficult childhood and young adulthood, during my addiction, my abusive relationships, and my recovery. I now realize that fight in me doesn't just serve me, it serves others as well, when I stand up and speak on behalf of people who have been abused or experienced Adverse Childhood Experiences (ACEs), and all sorts of unspeakable trauma. I also use my voice and fighting spirit to stand up for those fighting alcohol and substance abuse disorders. I understand intimately what they are up against—not just the disorders, but the stigma and shame that comes with it. I understand that they are fighting for their lives. They are doing all they can to live and fight back the demons and suffering from enduring a lifetime of pain. Again, I use my voice and fighting spirit to stand up for women who find themselves in abusive relationships—who tried to find solace and peace in what they thought was a loving relationship but ended up becoming a nightmare.

The reality is the things that break us also make us. In fact, they make us whole again. But they can also destroy us too, like Kryptonite, if we don't wrangle them in and learn how to transmute them or transform them into something good.

For example, the fighting spirit I have truly doesn't know when to stop! It can become a bit dangerous if left unchecked. As women, we all tend to push ourselves beyond our capacity. We abuse ourselves in all sorts of socially acceptable ways. We work out too hard. We work long days. We sacrifice sleep in the name of our hustle. We push and push and push ourselves beyond the brink.

I remember right after having my c-section, I was up and out of my bed, walking up and down the halls. I remember thinking I was so strong and so much better than all the women lying in bed—resting or in pain. They had every right to rest, to heal, to take what they needed. But in my mind, ever since I can remember, I have been a fighter. I felt, *I must get up. I must keep going. I must keep fighting. Pain and all other human emotions and sensations be damned! I am a Superwoman! I can do anything!* And in many ways, I could do it. But that didn't make it right, and it didn't make the women who couldn't do it weaker than me. In fact, sometimes it takes great strength to say no, to step back, and to rest. That kind of strength my heart wants to learn.

In 2023, I was preparing for my first international pageant. I was doing three intense workouts a day—Orangetheory classes, running more afterwards, and lifting weights. I was also taking care of my boys, working, and writing this book. I kept going and pushing myself. My husband warned me over and over: "Celia, you're doing too much."

You don't even have to guess what happened next. Surprise, surprise, my back went out for the first time in my entire life. I could barely sit down; the pain was so severe. This time the pain I felt in my backside wasn't because of my stepfather's or someone else's abuse—*it was my own!* I pushed myself too hard.

Now, I am not saying don't get out of your comfort zone or don't push yourself. What I am saying is to listen to your body. Listen to your soul. Ask yourself: *Why am I doing this? What do I have to prove and to whom? Am I really doing this for me? Or am I doing it because I care about what others think of me? Am I doing it to prove someone wrong? Like the old: "I'll show them!" Am I doing this because the little girl inside me is still trying so desperately to be seen, heard, and held?*

Succumbing to pain can be a curse too. Letting pain and excuses get in the way of your recovery and growth is a common path for many of us. It's easy to point the finger and blame my mother for everything that happened in my life, but part of my growth and healing was realizing she too needed healing. She too didn't have all the tools and skills. I could have blamed my father for leaving me, and not protecting me from abusive stepfathers, but that wouldn't have helped me heal. Our healing and growth come when we realize what happened to us isn't our fault, and when we make our healing our *own* responsibility.

No one else is going to do the work for us. The apologies may never come. But, when we heal ourselves, we don't need others to say, "We're sorry." We are gentle with ourselves. We forgive ourselves. We don't just push our pain aside. Instead, we acknowledge it, embrace it, and then transform it.

And pain, when it is alchemized and transmuted into something positive—when wielded correctly, this transformation can catapult you into the stratosphere.

Thankfully, I discovered the best way to transform my pain into a superpower was by channeling it into my fighting spirit and voice. For example, in most pageants, there is either a talent portion or a point in which you must speak to your audience. It's here, you get to show the audience and the judges who you really are—what you're really made of. In some ways, the judges want to see what your "superpower is" –what sets you apart from the others.

I know that my superpowers come from the pain I've endured for most of my life. More accurately, how I transmuted that pain and turned it to something I can use to help heal others. One of my superpowers has been this ability to heal—and to help others heal through sharing my story in the written word, in my podcasts, and on various stages.

There is no question in my mind, I would not be the person I am today had I not gone through so much pain. It was impossible to realize my worth and innate power when all I felt was darkness coupled with a void. It took me some time to take a hard look at my life and coping mechanisms. But it's here I found my power. For it is only when I faced my demons and overcame adversity that I discovered my true strength. And even then, I knew it was only a fraction of what is possible.

I can personally attest to the power one feels when they finally *break free*. Back when I was an addict, I would have said my past "broke me"—but now I see that it *broke me free* from the chains that had been binding me. I had to be torn down so I could rebuild myself and my life anew.

And then something even more magical happened. People who read or heard my story were healed as well.

They, too, felt inspired to share their own story and heal themselves and others in the process.

Imagine the power of one voice? One story? It will not only affect the people who hear it, but all the countless people who encounter those you have healed. It's like lighting a match in a full matchbook. Have you ever lit one match and used it to light another while still in the matchbook? The entire matchbook becomes engulfed in flames. Our light, when shared with just one other person, spreads exponentially. It can light up the entire world.

In a way, my ability to transform my pain into my fighting spirit and voice gave birth to healing and that too gave birth to a whole new set of superpowers: My empathy and intuitive abilities. You will find that when you move beyond the pain, a deeper level of empathy and intuitiveness exists deep within you.

And this is where things take off and the healing happens at a profound rate—for you and others. When you can just sit with someone and hear their story, without judgment, and have nothing to offer but a, "This is hard" or "I hear you" or "You have every right to be upset, hurt, traumatized" or "You did nothing wrong" or "I am always here for you," you are healing others. In fact, simply holding space for someone can be more healing than anything else you do, even better than giving advice or offering solutions.

Sharing our stories is powerful. But so is receiving others' stories with compassion and an open mind.

Everyone is truly fighting a hard battle we know nothing about. No one gets through this life without facing some loss or hardship. It's only when we can sit with each other, and our pain, can we truly begin to heal. The more honest we can become about our pain, the more open our hearts can be to receive others in their moment of need.

When we help others heal, we heal too.

Only someone who has been through what another is facing can know how to speak in the shape of their scars. Since I first began sharing my story to help others, people have shared things with me they haven't ever told anyone, and I have found a common theme within our dysfunctions. We haven't always had it easy. What seemed foreign, abnormal, and dysfunctional to those with healthy upbringings, was our reality. And that wasn't our fault.

Again, we are not to blame for what happened to us as children, clearly. But we are responsible for our own healing, our addictive behaviors, and how we react to situations that trigger us and pierce unhealed wounds. We also aren't to blame for our low self-esteem and lack of confidence.

Confidence is a skill you can learn. I have discovered this from my journey in pageantry. The comradery, support, and mentorship I have received from fellow contestants and coaches has been an incredible gift and helped me hone my natural gift of speaking and listening.

And healing can come in the most surprising ways too—at times when we least expect it.

When I was twenty-five, I was living at home with my mother. I had been in recovery and sober for five years. I was starting to find my voice, as well as a voice rising deep within me crying out to be heard. Once during a three-day writing binge, when I poured out my first memoir *Celia's Eyes,* I was struck with a fear that pierced me so psychically, I felt it deep within my bones. When I tried to speak, a little girl's voice came out and cried, "Mommy, mommy, please hold me." So, at twenty-five-years old, I crawled into bed with my mother where she held me like a baby. The little girl who wanted nothing more to be held, loved, and seen finally received her wish. My mom held me as I curled up against her in the fetal position. She held me until all the fear subsided.

I had been waiting for a lifetime to be held, and when I asked to be, she did. It was one of the most healing and transformative moments of my life. In the end, all of us are just small children longing to be held and loved. It took me many more years to figure out that grown-up Celia had to hold and love her inner child and all the pain that came with her too. But it was a start.

Today, I am still working on embracing that wounded and beaten little girl. I see her fierceness and strong fight in her and I am urging her on: *Keep at it! You got this! Don't give up!* I know she is with me too.

She is the one inside me pushing me past the finish line in triathlons. She is the one who gets up in the middle of the night to care for a sick child. She is the one closing deals and making record sales. She is the one using her voice to speak out on behalf of those struggling and hurting. She is the one crowning me Queen whether I win or lose a pageant. She is right there inside me, my biggest cheerleader, giving me my biggest, warmest, and tightest hug.

I recently learned a term called "cognitive reframing." It's when you teach your brain to look at situations and people differently. When I was a child and even a young adult, I never knew about this term. However, I realize now, I instinctively did it for my own sanity. I looked at everything that had gone wrong in my life and found the gift in it when I wrote my first book. I believed God was sharing his perspective with me. Yes, the Divine can speak to us directly. To this day, it is my truth that I was predestined for all the pain I have endured, because God knew I was strong enough to live through it. God gave me the gift to speak about it and then pave the way for others. If it's a lie, it's a beautiful one. And I do sleep more soundly with a purpose. That is certainly better than the alternative—living in resentment and bitterness. It rots you from the inside out. Life isn't fair sometimes. And when it isn't, as much as it hurts, we must move on and gracefully let go.

I believe that we come here with a purpose. The goal is to live up to our potential and fulfill our soul's purpose. God's gift to us is our potential. How are we going to give back? I was sent here to experience hell on earth on so many different levels so people would listen to me. Jesus was my hero growing up. Maybe he is my spirit guide. I haven't met any others, but I can say, I have met him once or twice. He did the same thing. His life was a sacrifice so we can be confronted with forces in our dreams and fearlessly say, "I rebuke you in the name of Jesus." Whether it's the power in the word Jesus or our belief or both, the fear goes away. The oppression stops.

My ability *to transform my pain into power* is truly a superpower. And it can be yours too if you embrace it. You may not have the same gifts as me. You may not be great with words or with speaking, but you may be an excellent listener, hugger, lover, grower, or match lighter. We all have gifts. We all have something inside of us that the pain whetted and honed—and eventually formed us in a way to pierce the hearts of others.

Some of us became vigilant as children and are keen observers today. We see everything—we see the pain in others' eyes—and we can help when no one else even notices. Some of us had to defend our siblings or ourselves, and we're wonderful protectors. We are excellent providers and accomplished at all sorts of things.

Every single one of us came here with a purpose—to use our God-given gifts to love and heal ourselves and others. How we choose to do it is up to each of us to find it. But it starts with embracing your own story.

I know that by telling my own story, I have only deepened my healing. And it is my deepest wish that others do too.

Fix Your Own Crown/Exercises

1. Could you view your own pain as a gift? As a superpower? If you are having trouble, can you think back to one of your first painful memories and "reframe it" like I did? I looked back at little wailing and kicking Celia fighting to be heard, and saw that as a wonderful gift, and one that served me well throughout my entire life. What served you during your most difficult moments as a child?
2. What about this gift, if not balanced or transmuted properly, can cause you more suffering (or has)? For example, my fighting spirit can run me right into the ground. It can also harden me a bit to the suffering of others. Sometimes, I don't realize just how tough I am and that others might not have the same talents or gifts.
3. Write a short story about your first memory, and how you see that as a superpower today.
4. Share that story with someone else who is also on their healing journey.

CHAPTER

Ten

Love Waits for You, Queen

So many of us waste years of our lives seeking outside validation and never feel fulfilled. We never feel the praise and achievements are enough. The reality is we are all inherently whole. We don't lack a thing. Accomplishments and support aren't the missing ingredients, *we are*. We have lost ourselves somewhere along the way.

We were born loved and complete with nothing here on this earth that we needed to earn. We instinctively knew this before the trauma came upon us. Just look at how innocent children carry themselves. We were there, too! And just like before our souls came here, as we are in this moment with no church doors or gurus in sight, we still have the same access to God—our Creator, Healer, the Divine. We were made with love, we come from love, and each of our God ordained purposes I believe involves us loving—ourselves and each other.

It was the most romantic of all gestures. Dane promised me he would love me until all the holes in my heart were filled on our second date, and he has. But as much as he tried to fill them all himself, it wasn't his work to do. No one else can fill the void inside of us. They can attempt to like my husband desperately tried to with me. But in doing so, it nearly destroyed him trying to save me. You see, no one else is the medicine—as much as we want them to be.

But what's even better? We are the medicine. We hold the keys.

Dane poured into me with everything he had to try and rescue me, protect us, and salvage our family. It did make me feel loved, unconditionally. He met my worst, and he didn't run. And I did my deepest healing work with the environment of love and support that only he has ever offered me. In a way, I guess my husband has helped raise me.

The elation we feel from falling in love, feeling that love reciprocated, receiving praise, earning achievements, doting parents, getting that guy you like, loyal husbands, or your child's snuggles isn't permanent. These feelings don't carry us through each moment, day in and day out. That's why I once struggled with feeling empty, despite having a picture-perfect life.

There is a place within you where you can return to love and return to God at any moment if you feel like you're struggling or stuck—and that is your heart. Some say it's an inside job to find the love accessible to each of us, but there's isn't anything new to find. It's already yours, but you must be willing to go within and not everyone is up for meeting themselves. Maybe they fear what they will find or what they will feel. This is why I ran for years. I do not judge you if you are there. I was you. It's as simple as surrendering, which I guess we both know isn't always that easy.

I also find God in what psychologists call the "flow state." Some experience this when they paint, draw, dance, play chess—I find it when I write. Think, what do you enjoy doing so much so that time stands still when you are engaged in the activity? You don't feel the compulsion to check your phone or scroll through social media.

I also find it when I immerse myself in nature and go on a hike, or when I facilitate my "Lead with Love workshops" where I am helping someone else by simply sharing that which was once so painful and shameful without tears. Those moments are evidence that my pain was transformed into *His* power to help others. I feel the flow state when I compete in beauty pageants where I share my testimony with judges and on stages in front of thousands whether watching in person or online. I experience a flow state when I prepare a TEDx talk or speech for a fundraiser. When I stand in front of an audience to speak, time slips away.

Imagine using everything you had ever been through for a greater purpose. I see many of you already doing this. How can we ever feel stuck for too long when we feel so much joy in serving or creating? For you, you may find it when you create by either cooking, sewing, or designing. Maybe you enjoy beauty pageants, too? Maybe they aren't for you. But only you know what it is that speaks to you. And whatever that is, seek God there too.

Access to Divine love has been in us the whole time, and it's just been there waiting for us to stop running. It's like Dorothy in the *Wizard of Oz*. The power was in her all along to return to her home. And we, too, have the power to return home to ourselves—to our loving and whole nature. We can come home any time we wish. He would wait forever for us, Queen.

It took me a few dark nights of the soul to realize that I didn't need someone to place a crown on my head to feel like a Queen—in other words, to feel worthy. Even my sense of self-worth had to come from me. In fact, someone did place a crown on my head, and because my insides didn't match with what was on the outside, I still didn't feel worthy of love. I felt worse.

You can have your passion and your purpose. You can do all the work with energy healers, coaches, and your inner child, but if you can't recognize that you're worthy of love—from yourself—then something will always feel off.

YOU ARE A QUEEN

You can be married to the best man in the universe, have beautiful children, a wonderful job, and be crowned Mrs. Tennessee, but still feel disconnected, still feel like you need to drink alcohol or have countless likes on Instagram to feel worthy. Nothing outside of you is ever going to fill the void inside of you. No magic number of likes will feed your hunger for your own self-love.

Every time you look at yourself in the mirror, I urge you to say, "Thank you, God. You're doing a good job." I overheard one of my five-year-olds, Preston, telling himself, "I love you," in the mirror last week. I thought it was the cutest thing, but it also made me very proud. I told him that is exactly what he should be doing. We are supposed to love ourselves.

I was twenty-five years old when I looked my own self in the eyes and tried this healing technique for the first time. I immediately burst into tears. I had either been shaming that girl who needed to hear that I loved her for the past, or telling her through my actions that I didn't love her for years. She desperately needed to hear it, and not only that, but for me to show it so she could begin healing. And she still needs it today. Try it for yourself. You deserve your love as much as anyone else.

I encourage you to experience love for yourself without relying on an external source or feeling. It's accessible to each of us. Everyone is worthy of love, part of the Divine, part of each other. *Love Waits for You*—for me, for all of us.

Straighten Your Crown Exercises:

- Recognize you are born of love, created in love, and no matter what you do in this life, you are still loved.
- Realize love for yourself will not come from an external source. No dream guy is going to give it to you, no friend group is going to give it to you, no amount of money, fame, or accomplishments can do it either.
- Write and say the affirmation, repeatedly, "I love me. I have enough. I do enough. I am enough. I am loved. And love is always inside me. God waits for me to open my heart and receive."

CHAPTER

Eleven

A Queen Walks the Walk

There is a point in every pageant contestant's journey when they must put on their platforms, slip into their heavily beaded gown, and sashay across the stage strutting their stuff. This is where you show off your most prized possession in a beauty pageant, your confidence. This is what can set you apart from those who wish for the courage to put themselves out there in this way and the ones who mask their insecurities with arrogance.

True confidence cannot be imitated. It must be earned through effort, practice, and time. Sometimes, all you can do is fake it until you make it, and that's better than not challenging yourself at all. That's how I got through my first pageant, the earlier days of speaking on stage, and the beginning of my recovery. However, if I were a judge after having met (and had ultimately learned to love) all the many unhealed versions of myself, I would be able to detect false confidence a mile away. There is a distinction. I have clearly sensed the difference within me as I have grown in self-confidence.

The pageant walk is made to look easy, but it is hard work to get it down. It takes hours upon hours of practice. We're not used to walking around in six-inch heels on a slick and sometimes bumpy stage without almost breaking our ankles. Even though I am somewhat of a seasoned pageant participant, it still takes a lot of training leading up to a competition to feel satisfied with my walk—with plenty of room remaining to further improve.

The process of nailing down your walk feels a lot like when you wake up to your true self and begin facing your trauma for the first time. It's akin to wearing a new pair of stilettos. It will feel awkward and uncomfortable. You will feel uneasy. You're going to feel a little wobbly and shaky. It's challenging work, and it takes a lot of practice. But you must get into those platforms every day and strut the highest version of yourself across the world's stage. You must keep at it, even when you mess up—and *you will mess up and fall.* Lord knows, I have fallen.

When you embark on the journey of healing your trauma, you must not only anticipate setbacks but have a mind that looks forward to who you will become once on the other side. Find the beauty in the fact that both your joy and your grief can coexist as you heal. Pushing it down and numbing our feelings may ease the pain, but we will one day wake up and find ourselves in a cage of our own making. To the extent we have faced our pain and fully processed it, that is the extent we will feel pure joy. That is the only way to get back to our pure, childlike state.

There is a verse I have always held onto from the Bible that speaks of pride coming before the fall. My deep sense of pride gets me every single time. We already know that I was not in the best place mentally when I competed in my first national pageant in November of 2021. Ok, we also know that is an understatement. I was barely holding it together. But thank goodness, I had already been humbled many times in my past or I might not have recovered as well as I had from such a humiliating moment.

Part of the national competition in Vegas included a costume portion where we represented our state. I wore a red bodysuit stoned with jewels and a flowy red cape that cascaded down like a waterfall when held up properly. I was representing a waterfall in Chattanooga, TN—Ruby Falls. As I was smiling and prancing across the stage during the preliminary competition—which by the grace of God only the final competition was live streamed—the announcer said, "She is the love story of the south. She *is* Ruby Falls!" The second he said the word *falls,* my right heel slipped on the sheer fabric from my cape. I plunged from my six-inch platforms directly down to the stage. I have been told it was the most graceful near tumble anyone has ever seen. And that I must be an athlete for how I controlled it. There was a knot on my knee for months from where I had descended to the ground. Thankfully, I was quick to catch myself and only my right knee made an impact. I immediately stood back up, smiled at the audience who were graciously cheering—for the emotional support I needed, it felt—and I kept strutting.

Once backstage, I shared with Mrs. South Carolina what had happened. She gave me her sunglasses to wear to hide my tears. Then I checked my phone to open a text from Dane, *You were a Ruby Fall!* Even in the middle of me crying from feeling embarrassed—but mostly from knowing any shot at winning was likely over—I was able to let out a giggle. My husband always brings humor and light-hearted energy to make me feel better when I need it most.

Much later, people from the audience who had met me in the elevator had even asked if it was intentional because of how it happened right as the announcer said the word "*fall.*" I just laughed it off with them. Afterall, what else can you do but laugh at yourself?

When you are walking this new walk—filled with self-love, intention, and integrity—you need to keep your sense of humor. We all mess up. Having the ability to laugh at yourself and being able to take yourself lightly is the key to sustaining your transformation. If you can't laugh at yourself, then you won't find anything in life to laugh about.

Looking back at my husband's recording of this symbolic moment, you can hear the gasp of air from the audience. It was if everyone in the room suddenly felt the surge to grab my hand in hopes of catching me before I had collapsed on stage. Also, if I am honest with myself, I didn't think to rehearse. This was partly due to me being so new to pageants or performing in any way, but the other piece of this reflected my pride. I didn't try the platforms on with the costume or bother walking across at least the carpet of my hotel room. If I had, I would've discovered that my cape *not only* needed to be held up to emanate a flowing waterfall, but to also not slip on it. It was a simple fix that I had nailed by the time the final competition that was filmed rolled around that evening. I did *not* make that same mistake twice.

Although I might have looked lovely, my heart was a wreck. I wasn't being honest with myself about my drinking or the emotional affair. I hadn't even begun to truly love myself. I hadn't even acknowledged my trauma, let alone processed it. I was full of pride, and I was brought to my knees, a recurring theme in my life. It always hurts my ego when I fall, whether *literally* or figuratively, but it frees my soul and for that I am grateful.

I have learned to reflect and consider the bigger picture—perceiving what doesn't meet the eye has helped me make sense of what has ever wounded me. The deeper I look, the further I see. This was a tool in my survival kit that I continue to use today. We each have this gift; we only access it differently. It is our intuition.

I know now, to "walk the walk," means to practice it every day. To not fear obstacles, failures, or falling backwards, but to expect them. Then, plan to get yourself back up, not be too prideful, trust the Divine Queen within, and get excited about the next version of you that will be revealed once you overcome it. Just keep walking. And eventually, it becomes muscle memory!

Straighten Your Crown Exercises:

- Be consistent—even when you feel shaky and wobbly.
- Embrace the falls—learn from them and get up and keep going.
- Have a sense of humor—look at yourself as if you are a child learning to walk—it takes baby steps. No one gets it right the first time.
- Don't get too self-righteous or prideful, no matter how accomplished you feel—you still need to practice.

CONCLUSION

Claim Your Title and Wear Your Crown with Pride

In the pageant world, it's custom for the reigning Queen to bestow the crown on the new queen's head. But, in real life, no one can make you feel like a "Queen" or crown you—that, we've already established, comes from within. And the only way to do that is to declare yourself a Queen. You must believe with your body, mind, and soul—that it is your birthright. You already wear the only crown that you can take with you—an eternal crown.

You were born of love, and you didn't have any control of the things this life threw at you. But you made it out of your dark night of the soul, had patience, forgave yourself, confronted your shadow, learned new ways to care for yourself, found your passion and purpose, *transformed your pain into power*, realized *love waits for you* and was in you all along, walked the walk, and so all there is left to do now is to claim your title, Queen. Own it and wear your crown with pride. A true Queen doesn't need someone to crown her. She doesn't need someone else to tell her what the end of her story is.

A true Queen writes her own ending.

I could have stayed a Little Princess Lost. I could have remained hooked on drugs, and never did any of the work to get me here. I could have kept telling myself or anyone who would listen that I was a victim of circumstance, and that it wasn't my fault. I could have ended up dead. But I chose to rewrite my own ending. I chose to be a Queen.

I choose her daily.

Maybe I was a lot like you. I bought every book I could, listened to every podcast, tried every modality to figure out a way to come back home to myself. Although I have reconnected with myself and rediscovered my inherent worthiness, I choose to still see myself as a work in progress. It's a decision I stand by to remain on this path dedicated to my personal development and healing. The longer I live my life in this way, the more I expand each day. Why stop now when we can keep growing?

You purchased this book because you, like me, are a seeker—your soul is crying out desperately for you to find answers. Deep down, you know you are a Queen, too. You have been through so much and it is this place of surrender that you have a shot at change—at reaching your full potential. This is your opportunity to make right any wrongs and wake up at 90 years old with peace and not regret.

This is *your* chance. This is an invitation to heal and rewrite your story. What do you want to write? You are already Queen in my eyes. You were born one.

My platform and nonprofit is called "Lead with Love." It was born from my healing journey and a desire to offer a light at the end of the tunnel for those struggling. I also want to inspire these individuals and those that care for them to lead with love and compassion versus judgment. That is the *only* way they have a shot at transformation.

When I compete, I give a rose quartz crystal with a note to each of my fellow contestants. The crystal symbolizes love, healing, and compassion. I include this quote, "You've already won for the woman you've become." Because I know that they must have each faced remarkable challenges and overcome them to possess the strength to open themselves up in such a vulnerable way.

A sister in pageantry told me once, "Your story isn't for everyone, but there's a story within it for everybody." You may not have gone through the exact same things I have, but not one of us gets through this life without a dark night of the soul or two (or five or six, etc.). *You are a Queen* in my book, and I know the same goes for me. I know I've already won in the eyes of God for the woman I've become. No crown bestowed on me from someone other than the Creator of this Universe is going to tell me that. I *know* I am a Queen. A Queen of my own heart, and I can do *anything*. And so can you!

Straighten Your Crown Exercises:

- Own it! You are a Queen!
- Now believe it and go rewrite your own ending.

Epilogue

During the same snow and ice storm of 2022 that was the miracle I had needed for my marriage, a thick layer of ice had developed on the top of our house. When it had started warming up, it had caused a large sheet of ice to slide off and crash down on my favorite type of tree since childhood, our Magnolia, leaving nothing but a stump behind. We thought it had died.

The other afternoon while Dane was watering our new trees the landscaper had planted, I noticed a magnolia tree and asked, "Did they also plant us a new magnolia tree?"

He then asked me, "Do you remember the storm from a couple of years ago?"

I thought, *How could I forget?* But instead responded, "I do."

He continued, "This is the same magnolia tree that was cut down to its near roots, but it grew back. This tree is a miracle. It shouldn't have survived." He then pointed to the scar on the base of its trunk from where it had almost lost its life. My eyes welled up with tears. I looked at my magnolias beginning to bloom and thanked God for more evidence that he is always with me. I only must perceive the signs and symbols.

I look for a loving God in everything I do. It's how I have healed realizing, "Yes, life can be hard. It was unbelievably unfair to me and countless others, but everything we go through can be used by God for our greater good." I really believe that everything happens *for* us not to us. No, you can't be insensitive and share with someone in grief that they have lost their child for a reason. Nor is it easy to believe this when you are overwhelmed by grief yourself.

But once you resurface
Only after you become
A Believer in his image
Of God—his only son

You will find all along
The pain—it served you well
The dreaming kept you alive
Now in his presence, you may dwell

In his presence, I delivered an eighteen-minute long TEDx talk where I essentially retraumatized myself the entire time without crying. Every time I rehearsed, I got emotional, but not during the event. I know when I speak on any stage, at schools, or facilitate one of my Lead with

Love Workshops, my role is to be a quiet strength for those in the audience who are grieving from me verbalizing the words they are unable to yet express. I can now share my story in any setting and not get emotional. This hasn't always been the case and is proof that whatever God is leading me to do is working.

Don't think I didn't suffer afterwards though. I wrote the poem below four days later as I sobbed uncontrollably. I had done enough work to know my body wouldn't stay there. However, I needed to acknowledge and express my pain. I needed to let the grief LEAVE. Poetry and writing have served as an outlet for accomplishing this.

The flood of tears we fear
We run—we fight the feeling of silence
The trauma, its healing?
Feels like grieving

It's the ache that doesn't bleed
From a loss that never leaves
In facing it—the naming of it?
We find the path to breaking free

We only need one hand to hold
We only need to be known
We do not have to be afraid
We are more powerful than our pain

As we feel our way out of the darkness
Where we can soothe our heart's return home to light
Know it was the flood of tears which we feared
Who walked us back home within the feeling of silence

Weeks after my first TEDx talk, beyond the other side of that dark cloud, I was lighter, and more healed than ever. Sometimes I ask God why he's keeping me here in my past as if I didn't already know. The answer is the more and more I go there, back to that hell for others, the less and less it hurts me. It gets worse before it gets better. But that's how he led me to heal myself. The day it stops hurting won't be the day he leads me to stop sharing my story. It will just be the day my wounded parts stop trying to get out of it asking why. My story is one that must be told because like my pageant sister said, there's a story within it to help everyone.

I can give myself credit for making significant progress—where the most painful pieces to process are behind me. But I am too smart to say I have healed; I have made that mistake and paid that price. My hard-earned humility instead will tell you there isn't an ending to this—there are only layers upon layers to continue digging through and unraveling—slowly and gracefully.

I believe that God guided me to pageantry. It was a calling that would unveil my true purpose—my ministry. It would shine a light on all I had left to heal. I had a book to unbury with a brand-new, untold story. I also carried some rough edges that needed to be refined.

Pageantry has also gifted me with a village of women who have helped emotionally support me as I have healed and empowered me to find—but most importantly— *use* my voice. You might think that it would be the people I have met through pageantry who would have told me, "You better hide your past." But this community says, "Embrace it. And use it to help others."

The most vulnerable I have ever been, I scored the highest with judges. The first time I competed I cried with one of them during the interview, and I got choked up on stage during the final question. They received my vulnerability with open arms. The second time that I placed the highest, I shared my story again—which at this moment was the last time I competed. I placed First Runner Up at an international pageant. By then, I did not cry, nor did I stutter. I spoke with the power from God's Holy Spirit in my voice, not pain.

I did not win, but I won.

I had healed enough by then to know I needed to make it less about me and my ego in that interview room. I considered the lasting impact and the ripple effects from sharing my story. You just never know what that other person across from you could be going through. I needed to let them see me, my past and all, so they could see to believe with their own eyes the redeeming power of God's love.

When I ask the Holy Spirit for help, I find it easier to think and communicate from the heart, much like Jesus would. I also speak with more strength. As much as my interview was about putting my best foot forward in hopes of winning, I redirected that energy towards what I could do for the soul across from me if I set my fear of being judged harshly aside. This is how I upheld poised communication about my journey, despite my challenging and unrefined past.

No matter what I decide to do next in pageantry, I have been transformed. Like everything in life, you get back what you put in and you harvest the results of your efforts. It isn't shining bright or sharing what is dear to your heart on a stage that is toxic. It is what that light reveals within us that hurts—whether we win or lose. And we can choose to stay there, or we can choose to heal.

Healing through pageantry was a part of my destiny to the same degree as my writing and ministry. They have been deeply interwoven. The poem I will share with you at the end states "I will crown your beautiful hair." I believe God gave me that poem to comfort me while knowing one day he would lead me to pageants, which would lead to my healing, and would then lead to my ministry he spells out in the poem. He knew I would then be called to write this book, and that in the end, circle back and see that the only crown I ever needed was his. And it's always been *mine*.

I am forever a Queen who knows and owns her worth. Now, all I want is to give to you what I have been given—which is his love. This is so that you, too, can heal and feel free to take up space, shine, look others in the eye, and ultimately live a life aligned with his purpose. So that you remain ready and available to continuously receive whatever it is he has in store. If *I* can get here, so can you.

Thank you for reconnecting to your heart even if it hurts—*especially* if it hurts. This is how we come home to ourselves. And it's there that we find everything we need. But this is the only beginning. Until our next time together.

With Love,

Celia

Ending Poem

This poem was given to me two months after I had written my first book, *Celia's Eyes*. It was March 25, 2011, and I was living in Chattanooga, Tennessee. I was working one afternoon and suddenly felt compelled to write. I grabbed the closest thing I could find to write on as it surged out of me. This is the only piece I have ever written by pen. For years, I would read these words and weep. As much as they were a gift and written for me, they can be true for you, too.

At the time of the poem, I identified as a "recovering drug addict." I am proof that you may always have an intense nature to regulate or a wounded self to master if this is an area you struggle with, but you don't have to always be "recovering." You, too, may reclaim what the locusts have eaten. You can find your way back to the real you.

Regardless of what you are healing from, it is a lifelong journey and commitment. But as you allow God's love to lead you, you will be able to Lead others with Love, too.

Serving others in this way—*that* is how you feel your pain transform into your power. This is how you beautifully heal.

Her Heart Broke Her Free

The worst is over now
Cry your tears of relief
Do you hear the trumpet sound?
It should bring you to your knees

There's always a hidden purpose
You could never comprehend
Not until it is over
Will you ever see the end

What He does
There's a reason
And the pain inflicted?
Wait Love, in due season

Don't trust the feelings
They surely never last
Such as what hurts
This too shall pass

And once you resurface
Only after you become
A Believer in His image
Of God, His only Son

You will find all along
The pain—it served you well
The dreaming kept you alive
Now in His presence, you will dwell

You know, maybe that's all He wanted
All along, after all
Was you, His beauty, His Bride
To Himself, without the walls

So yes, He broke you down
He tore your world apart
Then put you back together
And blessed you with a better start

For He knew your heart's desire
Wasn't what you were seeing
So He changed all that you saw
And left you with a new beginning

He left you raw
He left you bare
He added His majesty
And crowned your beautiful hair

With His love, His kind of beauty
No words could ever express
Yes, He destroyed what was my Dear
But He did it only to bless

YOU ARE A QUEEN

He knew you would be thankful
For He knew He made you smart
And that after the storm was over
You would have Jesus' kind of heart

And what you suffered
You'll never know again
My Child, I have given you a voice
A special voice that only spends

What you say will heal
What you say will touch
Now you're my kind of beautiful
Now you're my kind of loved

I promise you will have
What you saw in your dream
For I know your taste
And I'm working behind the scenes

Your mission is to fulfill
Your assignment is to speak life
In the hearts of those you love
For vengeance is always Mine

Forget what was
Prepare for that ahead
Stick to the script
Never fear, never dread

You will be made ready
You will shine bright
You will get through this
For I am by your side

I am in your heart
I am in your head
I am in your spirit
For I was never dead

I am all you dream
I am what you seek
I am all you want
I am who you need

Who has loved you more?
Who has ever filled?
Who has never hurt you?
Who has only healed?

You can't deny what is
What was or what will be
You can't deny the facts
For that's not reality

You don't need to be validated
You don't need to be told you're okay
You only need my Words in your heart
You only need Me to bless your day

YOU ARE A QUEEN

No one else matters
Not in the way I do
No one else cares
Not how I love you

So why won't you come
To the giver of Life
Partake and absorb
Why He came to die?

Your soul only needs
What only He can give
None of your searching
Will ever fulfill like this

You want to be free?
You want what lasts?
You want to be made whole?
Well it's in your very grasp

It's all about a choice
A getting real to oneself
A decision only you can make
You'll never run from death

His Life is forever
What He did was a big deal
If you knew what was good for you
You'd get down and you'd kneel

It's not about religion
It's not about who's who
It's not about who's watching
This is about you

This is your future
This is your now
This is for those you love
This is for us all somehow

I finally get
I finally am one who sees
I'll practice what I preach
I'll forever believe

He fixed me
I was a wreck
I was ugly
I was a mess

You'll never see the pictures
The past He put to death
He knows all my secrets
For He's been there every breath

I knew He was there
The time I won't get real
All I wanted was a tear
A cold heart's wish to feel

YOU ARE A QUEEN

It finally happened
And then I knew it was there
The same heart I grew up within me
This heart He never left

It was a turning point
One I will keep to me
It was just me and Jesus that day
For He promised not to leave

This man doesn't judge
He doesn't condemn
He makes a sinner beautiful
He is the One who gives

To her wretched self, once held captive
To the hate she bore inside
She never knew this was possible
Did you know she almost lost her life?

She only knew what she was told
She only knew what they would say
And all that wasn't too pretty
But they never knew her anyway

Even those related
The ones who impact the most
They never truly loved her
Not in the way she would've chosen

Has anyone truly known her?
Has she even known herself?
Has anyone once seen
A heart brought back from death?

This heart I recognize
I remember how it feels
I can say it's nothing new
And that sin doesn't always kill

This is what used to be
This is without what was
This is how it was meant for me
This is just what He does

So I'll get used to what He sees
I'll believe what He believes
And only because He says so
I will start to believe in me

I won't let you knock me down
I won't let you push me away
Because my heart won't ever come near you
In His arms I'll forever stay

And if He wants me to share
This love I hold inside
I'm out of the picture
My will for love dies

YOU ARE A QUEEN

It's His game, His idea
His agenda and His plan
I am a wreck at choosing players
So I'll let Him choose my future man

My hands this time are tied
My mouth is sewn shut
If He wants to open that door
He will only bring true love

None of what I have seen
None of what I've known
All of what He has
Will only bless my soul

Another sold out Believer
One who will understand
This heart and all that's in it
A love who'll forever stand

He'll never fall short
And he'll never leave
He'll be all that I dreamed
For he was meant for me

The timing I'm unsure
And the place unaware
But the beauty I can feel it
From the love of his care

But back to my Jesus
For now, I will stay
Glued to His promises
Day after day

Forever His
And forever will be
Year after year
Until made complete

And that won't be long
In eternity's eyes
So living for what's here
With my precious new life

I went a bit too long
So here is this ending
Take care and be blessed
With His love, I'll be sending

Acknowledgements

A heartfelt thank you to Marissa Marie Photography for capturing our family beach photos for the fourth consecutive year. You were so kind to include a few shots of me facing the ocean which helped bring my vision for this book cover to life. I appreciate your talent and dedication!

Thank you so much to Abdul Rehman for your incredible work on the layout of my book. Your creativity and attention to detail made a significant difference, and I'm grateful for your professionalism throughout the process. I couldn't have achieved this without your expertise.

Thank you to my writing coach from 2022-2023, Mary Hackett. Your unwavering support and compassion throughout this journey meant the world to me. You listened to my story, shared in my tears, and provided guidance that felt like a warm embrace. Though our paths have diverged, the impact you've had on my writing and personal growth will forever be cherished. Thank you for being a guiding light in this process.

And finally, thank you from the bottom of my heart to my amazing pageant sister, Lexi Spadaro, for generously donating your time to the project of editing my book. Your support and keen eye for detail have been invaluable. I am especially grateful for your willingness to write the foreword, adding your unique voice to my story. Your kindness and encouragement have meant so much to me!

Made in the USA
Columbia, SC
18 December 2024

f08d6b11-a203-4aef-9c57-b11e5c620d6aR01